the Voice™

NEW TESTAMENT

Step into the Story of Scripture

By

Ecclesia Bible Society

D0064117

THOMAS NELSON
Since 1798

NASHVILLE   DALLAS   MEXICO CITY   RIO DE JANEIRO

Printed in the United States of America

Contributors to *The Voice*

Editorial Review

Maleah Bell, B. C. Blackwell, Matthew Burleson, David B. Capes, James F. Couch, Jr., Amanda Haley, Kelly Hall, David Morgan, Merrie Noland, Chris Seay

Biblical Scholars

B. C. Blackwell, PhD; Joseph Blair, ThD; Darrell L. Bock, PhD; Beverly Burrow, PhD; David B. Capes, PhD; Alan Culpepper, PhD; Peter H. Davids, PhD; J. Andrew Dearman, PhD; Joseph Dodson, PhD; Brett Dutton, PhD; Dave Garber, PhD; Mark Gignilliat, PhD; Peter Rhea Jones, Sr., PhD; Sheri Klouda, PhD; Tremper Longman, PhD; Creig Marlowe, PhD; Troy Miller, PhD; David Morgan, PhD; Frank Patrick, PhD; Chuck Pitts, PhD; Brian Russell, PhD; Felisi Sorgwe, PhD; Kristin Swenson, PhD; Preben Vang, PhD; Nancy de Claissé Walford, PhD; Kenneth Waters, Sr., PhD; Jack Wisdom, JD

Contributing Writers

Ginny Allen, Lee Allen, Isaac Anderson, Eric Bryant, Beverly Burrow, David B. Capes, Cathy Capes, Daniel Capes, Don Chaffer, Lori Chaffer, Tara Leigh Cobble, R. Robert Creech, Greg Garrett, Christena Graves, Sara Groves, Charlie Hall, Amanda Haley, Kelly Hall, Greg Holder, Justin Hyde, Andrew Jones, E. Chad Karger, Tim Keel, Greg LaFollette, Katie Lerch, Evan Lauer, Paul Littleton, Todd Littleton, Phuc Luu, Christian McCabe, Brian McLaren, Donald Miller, Mike Morrell, Damien O'Farrell, Sean Palmer, Jonathan Hal Reynolds, Matthew Ronan, Chris Seay, Robbie Seay, Kerry Shook, Christopher R. Smith, Chuck Smith, Jr., Allison Smythe, Leonard Sweet, Kristin Swenson, Alison Thomas, Phyllis Tickle, Gideon Tsang, Matthew Paul Turner, Lauren Winner, Seth Woods, Dieter Zander

Other Contributors

Kipton Blue, Tyler Burkum, Steven Delopoulos, Jill Paquette DeZwaan, Marilyn Duncan, Brandon Graves, Andy Gullahorn, Steve Hindalong, Will Hunt, Kelly Jackson, Matthew P. Jones, Phil Keaggy, Russ Long, Maeve, Steve Mason, Sandra McCracken, Andrew Osenga, Kendall Payne, Rob Pepper, Holly Perry, U. J. Pesonen, Andrew Peterson, Jay Pfeifer, Jill Phillips, Robbie Seay Band, Jami Smith, Luke Sullivant, Amy Wallenbeck, Derek Webb, Matt Wertz

Preface

Any literary project reflects the age in which it is written. **The Voice** is created for and by a church in great transition. Throughout the body of Christ, extensive discussions are ongoing about a variety of issues including style of worship, how we distinguish cultural expressions from genuine expressions of faith, what it means to live the gospel, and how we faithfully communicate the essential truth of historic Christianity. At the center of this discussion is the role of Scripture. Instead of furthering the division over culture and theology, it is time to bring the body of Christ together again around the Bible. Thomas Nelson Publishers and Ecclesia Bible Society together are developing Scripture products that foster spiritual growth and theological exploration out of a heart for worship and mission. We have dedicated ourselves to hearing and proclaiming God's voice through this project.

Previously most Bibles and biblical reference works were produced by professional scholars writing in academic settings. **The Voice** uniquely represents collaboration among scholars, pastors, writers, musicians, poets, and other artists. The goal is to create the finest Bible products to help believers experience the joy and wonder of God's revelation.

Uniqueness of **The Voice**

About 40 different human authors are believed to have been inspired by God to write the Scriptures. **The Voice** retains the unique literary perspective of the human writers. Most English translations attempt to even out the styles of the different authors in sentence structure and vocabulary. Instead, **The Voice** distinguishes the uniqueness of each author. The heart of the project is retelling the story of the Bible in a form as fluid as modern literary works, yet remaining painstakingly true to the original Greek, Hebrew, and Aramaic texts. Accomplished writers and biblical scholars are teamed up to create an English rendering that, while of great artistic value, is carefully aligned with the meaning inherent in the original language. Attention is paid to the use of idioms, artistic elements, confusion of pronouns, repetition of conjunctions, modern sentence structure, and the public reading of the passage.

To help the reader understand how the new rendering of a passage compares to the original texts, several indicators are embedded within the text.

- **Standard type** denotes the dynamic translation that is the base all the elements are built on. It translates the many imprecise words that English translations have borrowed in their renderings: LORD, Christ, baptism, angel, and apostle. The process for each book began as negotiation between a gifted writer and scholars working in the original language. After that first phase, a few selected scholars carefully read the manuscript, comparing it to the original language, and evaluated the faithfulness to the text and the theological nuances of the translation. At the same time a publishing team ran consistency checks, copyedited the manuscript, and compared the rendering with the major existing English translations. A final acceptance process included each of the three groups impacting the translation: biblical scholarship, English writing competence, and publishing expertise.

- **Italic type** indicates words not directly tied to the dynamic translation of the original language. These words bring out the nuance of the original, assist in completing ideas, and often provide readers with information that would have been obvious to the original audience. These additions are meant to help the modern reader better understand the text without having to stop and read footnotes or a study guide.
- **Delineated material** expands on the theme found in the text. This portion is not taken directly from the original language and is set apart in a second color or a colored line, dividing it from the Bible text. It may include cultural, historical, theological, or devotional thoughts.
- **Screenplay format** is used to identify dialogue and to avoid the endless repetition of conjunctions, articles, and certain verbs. The speaker is indicated, the dialogue is indented, and quotation marks are avoided. This helps greatly in immediate comprehension of the situation for the user and in intensifying the dramatic presence during the public reading of Scripture. Sometimes the original text includes interruptions in the dialogue to indicate the attitude of the speaker or to show who is being addressed. This is shown either as a stage direction immediately following the speaker's name or as part of the narrative section that immediately precedes the speaker's name.

We follow the standard conventions used in most translations regarding textual evidence. **The Voice** is based on the earliest and best manuscripts from the original languages (Greek, Hebrew, and Aramaic). When significant variations influence a reading, we follow the publishing standard by bracketing the passage and placing a note at the bottom of the page, while maintaining the traditional chapter and verse divisions. The footnotes reference quoted material and help the reader understand the translation for a particular word. Words that are borrowed from another language and words that are not common outside of the theological community (such as "baptism," "repentance," and "salvation") are given expanded translations derived from more common terminology. For clarity some pronouns are replaced with their antecedents. Because Greek word order and syntax differ significantly from English, we have followed standard translation practices and altered these elements when necessary to help the reader achieve clarity in understanding Scripture and its meaning.

Our purpose in using these literary devices is to reveal the beauty of the Scriptures and to assist the reader in clearly and quickly understanding the meaning of the text. We are constrained to be faithful to these ancient texts while giving the present reader a respectful and moving experience with the Word of God.

A Different Translation Process

The Voice Bible is a different sort of translation. It combines the relative strengths of scholars who are experts in the original languages (in the case of the New Testament, Greek) and modern writers, musicians, and poets who are skilled in their use of English, our target language. Our idea was to set up a collaborative process whereby scholars and writers could work together to create a translation that was faithful and accurate to the original languages while at the same time beautiful and readable to our English-speaking audience. In some cases scholars and writers worked closely together; in others they worked at some distance or even anonymously. Members of the translation team from Ecclesia Bible Society and Thomas Nelson coordinated the overall process.

Whenever people render one language into another (whether ancient or modern), they are involved in translation. There are levels of formality in the translation process. Generally, these are described on a continuum between formal and functional equivalence. But these approaches are not followed strictly by any Bible translation team, and most translations must mix formal with functional elements in order to communicate clearly. Realistically, languages are too complex and fluid to be reduced to a single approach in translation. A strictly formal translation process will result in an unreadable text that obscures the meaning of Scripture rather than making it accessible. A strictly functional translation process will result in a text that might communicate to a reader well what the original text means but not what the original says.

With **The Voice** Bible we acknowledge the difficulties translation teams face and offer what might be described as a mediating position between the extremes. We describe our approach as "contextual equivalence." Recognizing that context is the most important factor in determining the meaning of a word, sentence, paragraph, or narrative, we have sought to create a Bible translation that preserves both the linguistic and the literary features of the original biblical text. A "contextual equivalent" translation technique seeks to convey the original language accurately while rendering the literary structures and character of a text in readable and meaningful contemporary language. This particular translation approach keeps in mind the smaller parts and the larger whole. In endeavoring to translate sacred Scripture, **The Voice** captures uniquely the poetic imagery and literary artistry of the original in a way that is beautiful and meaningful.

Two other related descriptors are used to situate a Bible translation in the field. Some claim their translations are "word-for-word" in contrast to those that are "thought-for-thought." Word-for-word translations generally claim to be more literal and therefore superior to those that are thought-for-thought. The critique is sometimes made that thought-for-thought translations reflect the interpretive opinions of the translators and are influenced by the contemporary culture more than word-for-word translations. This critique is not necessarily relevant, for these translation endeavors—whether from the so-called "word-for-word" (formal) or "thought-for-thought" (functional) translation philosophies—are only different in degree, not in kind.

There are four primary objections to these claims. First, every translation is an interpretation. Anyone who has studied translation theory recognizes that it is impossible for translators to get outside their skins and objectively render a text. The Italians say it bluntly: *tradutorre, traditore*—"The translator is a traitor." Even if it were deemed useful to design a computer program to translate mechanically the Scriptures into English, human subjectivity and judgment would still come into play in various ways; for example, choosing which texts to translate and deciding which English word to use to translate a specific

Greek word. Subjectivity and interpretive opinions are impossible to avoid in the translation process and do not necessarily have a negative impact on a translation.

This leads to a second objection regarding the nature of words and thoughts. The strict distinction between "word" and "thought" must be questioned. After all, a word is merely an expressed thought, whether spoken or written. This becomes clear when dealing with people who are fluent in multiple languages. When they have a thought they wish to express, they must choose which language, then which word or words, then which word order. There may be line of distinction between a thought and a word, but it is not a hard and fast line; it is at best a dotted line.

Third, words generally do not have a single meaning; they have a range of meanings—what linguists refer to as a semantic field. Even the translators of the King James Bible recognized that words do not carry the same sense every time they occur in a text (see preface to the 1611 edition). So, for example, how should one translate the Greek noun *dikaiosunē?* In one place the word might mean "justice," in another "righteousness," in another "equity" or "integrity," yet in another something that is "true" or "right." One must understand the context in which a word is used in order to render carefully its meaning in another language. This context is not just semantic but also historical and social. For example, our use of "God's Anointed" or "the Anointed One" as a translation of the title "Christ"—and in selected places expanded to "God's Anointed, *the Liberating King*"—captures something of the historical and social reality behind Jesus' identity. He is God's Anointed King who comes to liberate His people from sin, addiction, disease, oppression, and death.

To press this point even further, words don't just *mean* things, they *do* things. Words have both meaning and function; they function within clauses, sentences, paragraphs, and stories in ways that are different from the definition a person might find in a dictionary or lexicon. Beyond this, however, words also function in various ways to elicit emotions, actions, and responses from those who hear them. In order to translate a text well, one must consider not only what words mean but what they do.

Fourth, a word-for-word correspondence is difficult to maintain because translators may need multiple words in one language to express the meaning of a single word in another. Take for instance the Greek word *sōthēsetai* (Romans 10:13). Because of the way the English language works, it takes no fewer than four words to translate this single Greek verb: "he/she will be saved." Again, the context will reveal who will be saved, what salvation entails, and when it is realized.

When all of these factors are taken into consideration, **The Voice** represents a hybrid of the word-for-word and thought-for-thought approaches. In some places **The Voice** follows a word-for-word translation; in others it expresses the meaning more in a thought-for-thought approach. This is necessitated contextually both by the original language and by our target language (English). Responsibility to render the biblical languages carefully and to create a readable translation for an audience is not an either/or pursuit; a "contextual equivalent" translation seeks to be faithful and realistic to both tasks.

Another issue **The Voice** project team had to address involved inclusive language. Generally speaking, we have made no attempt to make **The Voice** gender neutral or gender inclusive. We have tried to follow the sense of the text and have made translation decisions based on the context. When, for example, Paul reminded the *adelphoi* ("brothers") of Corinth of the content of the gospel (1 Corinthians 15:1-8), it is unlikely that he intended to include the "brothers" and exclude the "sisters." Since the apostle adopted typical letter-writing practices of his day, his manner of addressing the community was likely determined by cultural mores. In such cases, we have decided to render the text "brothers and sisters." However, in texts where it is clear that the admonition is addressed to one gender and not the other, we have taken seriously the historical situation and utilized the appropriate masculine or feminine nouns and pronouns. The warnings against loose women in Proverbs 5–7, for example, are clearly aimed at young men. Furthermore, Proverbs 31 does not describe a remarkable partner or spouse but a remarkable woman who happens to also be a wife. This perspective respects the particular situations that gave rise to the texts in their original historical settings and does not seek to exclude (or include for that matter) those not being directly addressed by the biblical writers. Commentaries and proper exegesis can make reasonable application of texts across gender lines in ways translations cannot.

Finally, although **The Voice** Bible represents a new approach to Bible translation, we have intentionally avoided the tendency to use trendy language. Our goal was to capture the beauty and brutal honesty of the Scriptures in language that is timeless and enduring. In the process, we have come to recognize our profound indebtedness to the various strands of Christian tradition that have made these texts available. We stand in gratitude to a multitude of saints who gave their lives to preserve and transmit the Scriptures in their original languages from one generation to the next. We acknowledge the significant contributions made by the Reformers and their followers (not to mention their predecessors) to give us a common language and scriptural heritage in the English-speaking world. Although we have not always tried to imitate them, we have always learned from them. Our hope and prayer is that a new generation of people will encounter the Scriptures through **The Voice** and step into the story of Scripture.

Christ in This Translation

In its original Greek language the New Testament refers to Jesus hundreds of times as *Christos*. Most English translations of Scripture render this "Christ," which is not a translation but a transliteration. The unfortunate effect of this decision is that most readers mistake "Christ" as a kind of second name for Jesus. In fact, *Christos* is not a name at all; it is a title. It is a Greek translation of the Hebrew title "Messiah." So when the New Testament writers call Jesus "(the) Christ," they are making a bold claim—one of the central claims of the Christian faith—that Jesus is the Messiah. While there was no single expectation about the Messiah in Jesus' day, many of his contemporaries would have recognized the Messiah to be God's agent who comes in the last days to redeem God's people and repair our broken world.

While we understand that no single English word or phrase captures the richness of the term "Messiah," we made a strategic decision in **The Voice** to translate *Christos* and not simply to transliterate it. The root idea of *Christos* is derived from a Greek verb meaning "to anoint (with oil)." The act of anointing someone with oil is a way of setting that person apart for God's use. When people are anointed—kings and priests, for example—oil is poured over their heads, signifying God's Spirit coming upon them and empowering them for the tasks ahead. This is why we have decided to translate *Christos* as "God's Anointed," "the Anointed," or "the Anointed One," depending on context and narrative flow.

But there is another aspect of *Christos* we need to highlight. You see, according to tradition, the Messiah is to be a son of David, and as such he has a royal function to continue David's dynasty and to reign over a newly constituted kingdom. In order to become king, a person must have God's anointing. So from time to time, as we translate *Christos* as "God's Anointed," we have added the explanatory phrase "the Liberating King" to remind us of the primary mission and of the reason God elects and empowers Jesus in the first place. Jesus comes as the King of a new kind of kingdom and exercises His royal power to rescue and liberate His creation. Now this liberation takes place on various levels, all of which are related.

Not long after Jesus begins his public ministry, he returns to the synagogue in Nazareth—where He had grown up—and reads the Scripture portion that day from Isaiah 61 (Luke 4:18-19):

> The Spirit of the Lord the Eternal One is on Me.
> *Why?* Because the Eternal designated Me
>   to be His representative to the poor, to preach good news to them.
> He sent Me to tell those who are held captive that they can now be set free,
>   and to tell the blind that they can now see.
> He sent me to liberate those held down by oppression.
> *In short, the Spirit is upon Me* to proclaim that now is the time;
>   this is the jubilee season of the Eternal One's grace.

From the way Jesus responds to the reading that day, it is clear that He understands His Spirit-enabled work to be about proclaiming the good news, releasing exiles and other political prisoners, healing the sick, and freeing the oppressed—in a word, "liberating" the poor, the captive, the sick, and the marginalized from whatever threatens them. But there is more. The Scriptures declare that Jesus comes to liberate those made in His image from the power and penalty of sin, which is the reason God's good creation is so fouled up and disordered in the first place. In fact Paul tells the Romans that all creation has been damaged by sin and longs for the day when God's children are revealed and set free from the power of sin and death. When that day comes, creation itself will be liberated from its own slavery to corruption (Romans 8:18-25). By translating *Christos* as "God's Anointed, *the Liberating King*" on occasion we are reminded of the title's true meaning and emphasizing an important truth—namely this: that the extent of Jesus' kingdom as God's Anointed and the reach of His liberating work extend beyond our hearts, beyond our politics, beyond our world.

JOHN

Visitation of God's Son

By John, the apostle

According to tradition, this Gospel was written by John the apostle toward the end of his life from Ephesus in Asia Minor. Along with Peter and James, John was part of an inner circle of disciples closest to Jesus. Many interpreters think that "the beloved disciple"—a unique description in this book for one of Jesus' followers—refers to John. If so, John enjoyed a special relationship with Jesus that allowed him to offer a unique account of Jesus' life.

This Gospel is distinct from the other New Testament Gospels. Matthew, Mark, and Luke present the life of Jesus from a similar perspective. They share a number of parallel accounts, arrange them in a similar order, and use many of the same words and expressions. Because of their similarities, Matthew, Mark, and Luke are often called the Synoptic Gospels. "Synoptic" means "with the same eye" or "seeing together." The Gospel of John, on the other hand, contains only a little of the material found in the other Gospels. John takes us behind the scenes into Jesus' conversations with people and into long, often private talks He has with His disciples. Jesus is clearly a miracle worker in this Fourth Gospel, but His miracles are regarded as "signs" because they point to a greater reality, the reality of life—abundant and eternal—that has entered our world. Further, John makes many bold claims to Jesus' deity. For example, John includes a number of "I am" sayings spoken by Jesus (for example, "I am the bread that gives life," "I am the light of the world," and "I am the resurrection and the source of all life"). These statements associate Jesus with God's holy, unspeakable name and are implicit claims to His divinity. Plus, in John's theological prologue (John 1:1-18), the author calls Jesus the *Logos* ("the Voice") that preexists with God, is the agent of creation, and is made flesh for the world's salvation.

Another unique feature of this Gospel is its simplicity. Its language and grammar are easily grasped. Its ideas—while deeply symbolic and evocative—can be understood by people of all ages and experiences. It is filled with dualisms that emphasize the difference eternal life makes when it enters into the world: life and death, belief and unbelief, light and darkness, to name a few. For many people, the simplicity of this Gospel, with its intimate look at Jesus' life, makes it their favorite story of the Anointed One sent from God.

This Gospel begins not with Jesus' birth or John's baptism but with a deliberate echo of the creation story in Genesis. It takes us back before time began to the moment when God interrupts the silence and speaks the cosmos into existence. Only John's Gospel names Jesus as the *Logos* and declares that He existed long before time was measured. This Greek word carries a variety of meanings, all relating to the act of speaking. It could be translated "word," a thought that comes to expression, message, declaration, reason, or the content of preaching; most are found in various translations. It is clear that John means that *logos* is declared to all creation.

John's use of *logos* is unique and has often been rendered as "Word." While this is a useful translation, even a casual understanding demonstrates that "Word" reflects only part of its meaning. Most readers will interpret "word" as a unit of language—a combination of sounds generally spoken but also written—that carries meaning. To understand what John means, readers need something more than their cultural understanding of "word"; they need a new way of thinking about it. This is why we have chosen to offer another rendering, an interpretive, poetic translation, of what may be one of the most theologically loaded words in Scripture. Since *logos* essentially refers to the act of speaking or bringing thoughts to expression, we have decided to use the word "voice" to capture that reality. John declares that truth has culminated in the person of Jesus. No single word captures the complete meaning of *logos*, but "voice" has a number of advantages.

First, "voice" manifests the act of speaking. Voice is that which is spoken and that which is heard; it comes on both sides of any communication event, bridging the gap between sender and receiver. John intends that in Jesus God is speaking and revealing Himself to the world.

Second, a voice is distinct and personal. We can distinguish people from one another simply by their voices. In John 10 Jesus describes the fact that the sheep hear the voice of the shepherd when he calls and they follow, but they refuse to follow a stranger because they do not know his voice (John 10:1-5). John desires that we know Jesus as the Son of God and believe in Him personally as the Good Shepherd.

Third, "voice" is dynamic in that it reflects the robust and powerful activity of a living God. It is historical in that any act of speaking comes to expression and takes place in the real world as a "voice" calling, demanding a response. It challenges any notion that the Christian faith can be reduced to rules, propositions, or doctrines that can be merely believed or dismissed and not lived out in our lives. Since in Jesus God is speaking and revealing Himself to the world, and since in Jesus we hear the Voice of God, then this new reality changes everything so we, too, must change.

In the beginning

1 Before time itself was measured, the Voice was speaking.

The Voice was and is God.
²This *celestial* Word remained ever present with the Creator;
³His speech shaped the entire cosmos.
Immersed in the practice of creating, all things that exist were birthed in Him.
⁴His breath filled all things with a living, breathing light—
⁵A light that thrives in the depths of darkness,
blazes through murky bottoms.
It cannot and will not be quenched.

⁶A man named John, who was sent by God, *was the first to clearly articulate the source of this Light.* ⁷This *baptizer* put in plain words the *elusive mystery of the Divine Light* so all might believe through him. *Some wondered whether he might be the Light,* ⁸but John was not the Light. He merely pointed to the Light. ⁹The true Light, who shines upon *the heart of* everyone, was coming into the cosmos.

Jesus as the Light does not call out from a distant place but draws near by coming into the world.

¹⁰He entered our world, a world He made; yet the world did not recognize Him. ¹¹Even though He came to His own people, they

refused to *listen and* receive Him. [12]But for all who did receive and trust in Him, He gave them the right to be *reborn as* children of God; [13]He bestowed this birthright not by human power or initiative but by God's will.

[14]The Voice took on flesh *and became human* and chose to live alongside us. We have seen Him, enveloped in undeniable splendor—the one *true* Son of the Father—*evidenced in* the perfect balance of grace and truth. [15]John *the Baptist* testified about Him and shouted, "This is the one I've been telling you is coming. He is much greater than I am because He existed *long* before me." [16]Through this man we all receive *gifts of* grace beyond our imagination. [17]You see, Moses gave *us* rules to live by, but Jesus the Anointed offered *us* gifts of grace and truth. [18]God, unseen until now, is revealed in the Voice, God's only Son, *straight from* the Father's heart.

Before Jesus comes along, many wonder whether John the Baptist might be the Anointed One sent by God. But when Jesus appears in the wilderness, John points others to Him. John knows his place in God's redemptive plan: he speaks God's message, but Jesus is the Word of God. John rejects any messianic claim outright. Jesus, though, accepts it with a smile, but only from a few devoted followers—at least at first. Of course John is crucial to the unfolding drama, but he isn't the long awaited One sent to free His people. He preaches repentance and tells everybody to get ready for One greater to come along. The One who comes will cleanse humanity in fire and power, he says. John even urges some of his followers to leave him and go follow Jesus.

[19]The reputation of John was *growing*; and many had questions, including Jewish religious leaders from Jerusalem. [28]So some *priests and Levites* approached John in Bethany just beyond the Jordan River while he was baptizing *and bombarded him with questions:**

Religious Leaders: Who are you?

John the Baptist: [20]I'm not the Anointed One, *if that is what you are asking.*

Religious Leaders: [21]*Your words sound familiar, like a prophet's.* Is that how we should address you? Are you the Prophet Elijah?

John the Baptist: No, I am not Elijah.

Religious Leaders: Are you the Prophet *Moses told us would come?*

John the Baptist: No.

Religious Leaders: [22]Then tell us who you are and what you are about because everyone is asking us, *especially the Pharisees,* and we must prepare an answer.

[23]John replied with the words of Isaiah the prophet:

John the Baptist: *Listen!* I am a voice calling out in the wilderness. Straighten out the road for the Lord. *He's on His way.**

[24-25]Then some of those sent by the Pharisees questioned him again.

Religious Leaders: How can you *travel the countryside* baptizing* people if you are not the Anointed One or Elijah or the Prophet?

John the Baptist: [26]Baptizing with water is what I do; but the One *whom I speak of, whom we all await,* is standing among you; and you have no idea who He is. [27]Though He comes after me, I am not even worthy to unlace His sandals.*

The mystery of Jesus' identity occupies His contemporaries and will continue to occupy generations of believers for centuries to come. As the twelve journey with Him, it gradually becomes clearer who this man is, where He

* 1:28 Verse 28 has been inserted here to help retain the continuity of events. * 1:23 Isaiah 40:3 * 1:24-25 Literally, immersing, to show repentance * 1:27 Verse 28 has been moved before verse 20 to retain the continuity of events.

comes from, and how His existence will profoundly affect the rest of human history. The question of "Who is this man?" cannot be answered overnight.

---

²⁹The morning after *this conversation,* John sees Jesus coming toward him. *In eager astonishment,* he shouts out:

John the Baptist: Look! *This man is more than He seems!* He is the Lamb sent from God, *the sacrifice* to erase the sins of the world! ³⁰He is the One I have been saying will come after me, who existed long before me and is much greater than I am. ³¹*No one* recognized Him—myself included. But I came baptizing* with water so that He might be revealed to Israel. ³²As I watched, the Spirit came down like a dove from heaven and rested on Him. ³³I didn't recognize Him *at first,* but the One who sent me to baptize told me, "The One who will baptize with the Holy Spirit will be the person you see the Spirit come down and rest upon." ³⁴I have seen this *with my own eyes* and can attest that this One is the Son of God!

³⁵⁻³⁶The day after, John *saw Him again as he* was visiting with two of his disciples. As Jesus walked by, he announced again:

John the Baptist: Do you see Him? This man is the Lamb of God, *God's sacrifice to cleanse our sins.*

³⁷At that moment, the two disciples began to follow Jesus, ³⁸⁻³⁹who turned back to them, saying:

Jesus: What is it that you want?

Two Disciples: We'd like to know where You are staying. Teacher, *may we remain at Your side today?*

Jesus: Come and see. *Follow Me, and we will camp together.*

It was about four o'clock in the afternoon *when they met Jesus.* They came and saw where He was staying, *but they got more than they imagined.* They remained with Him the rest of the day *and followed Him for the rest of their lives.* ⁴⁰⁻⁴¹One of these new disciples,

Andrew, rushed to find his brother Simon and tell him they had found the One who is promised, God's Anointed *who will heal the world.* ⁴²As Andrew approached with Simon, Jesus looked into him.

Jesus: Your name is Simon, and your father is called John. But from this day forward you will be known as Peter,* the rock.

⁴³⁻⁴⁴The next day Jesus set out to go into Galilee; and when He came upon Philip, He invited him to join them.

Jesus: Follow Me.

Philip, like Andrew and Peter, came from a town called Bethsaida; *and he decided to make the journey with Him.* ⁴⁵Philip found Nathanael, *a friend, and burst in with excitement:*

Philip: We have found the One. Moses wrote about Him in the Law, all the prophets spoke of the day when He would come, and now He is here—His name is Jesus, son of Joseph *the carpenter;* and He comes from Nazareth.

Nathanael: ⁴⁶How can anything good come from *a place like* Nazareth?

Philip: Come with me, and see for yourself.

⁴⁷As Philip and Nathanael approached, Jesus saw Nathanael and spoke to those standing around Him.

Jesus: Look closely, and you will see an Israelite who is a truth-teller.

Nathanael (*overhearing Jesus*): ⁴⁸How would You know this about me? *We have never met.*

Jesus: *I have been watching you* before Philip invited you here. *Earlier in the day,* you were enjoying *the shade and fruit of* the fig tree. I saw you then.

Nathanael: ⁴⁹Teacher, You are the One— God's own Son and Israel's King.

Jesus: ⁵⁰Nathanael, if all it takes for you to believe is My telling you I saw you under the fig tree, then what you will see later

* 1:31 Literally, immersing, to show repentance   * 1:42 Literally, Cephas

will astound you. ⁵¹I tell you the truth: *before our journey is complete*, you will see the heavens standing open while heavenly messengers ascend and descend, *swirling around the Son of Man.*

2 Three days later, they all went to celebrate a wedding feast in Cana of Galilee. Mary, the mother of Jesus, was invited ²together with Him and His disciples. ³While they were celebrating, the wine ran out; and Jesus' mother hurried over to her son.

Mary: *The host stands on the brink of embarrassment; there are many guests, and* there is no more wine.

Jesus: ⁴Dear woman, is it our problem *they miscalculated when buying wine and inviting guests*? My time has not arrived.

⁵*But* she turned to the servants.

Mary: Do whatever my son tells you.

⁶In that area were six *massive* stone water pots that could each hold 20 to 30 gallons.* They were typically used for Jewish purification rites. ⁷Jesus' instructions *were clear*:

Jesus: Fill each water pot with water until it's ready to spill over the top; ⁸then fill a cup, and deliver it to the headwaiter.

They did exactly as they were instructed. ⁹After tasting the water that had become wine, the headwaiter couldn't figure out where such wine came from (even though the servants knew), and he called over the bridegroom *in amazement.*

Headwaiter: ¹⁰*This wine is delectable.* Why would you save the most exquisite fruit of the vine? A host would generally serve the good wine first and, when his inebriated guests don't notice or care, he would serve the inferior wine. You have held back the best for last.

¹¹Jesus performed this miracle, the first of His signs, in Cana of Galilee. *They did not know how this happened;* but when the disciples *and the servants* witnessed this miracle, their faith blossomed.

With a wedding as the setting of Jesus' first sign, John shows how

Jesus' ministry isn't limited to just "spiritual" things, but is His blessing for all of life.

¹²Jesus then gathered His clan—His family members and disciples—for a journey to Capernaum where they lingered several days. ¹³The time was near to celebrate the Passover, *the festival commemorating when God rescued His children from slavery in Egypt,* so Jesus went to Jerusalem *for the celebration.* ¹⁴*Upon arriving,* He entered the temple *to worship. But the porches and colonnades* were filled with merchants selling *sacrificial animals (such as* doves, oxen, and sheep) and exchanging money. ¹⁵Jesus fashioned a whip of cords and used it *with skill* driving out animals; He scattered the money and overturned the tables, emptying profiteers from the house of God. ¹⁶There were dove merchants *still standing around*, and Jesus reprimanded them.

Jesus: *What are you still doing here?* Get all your stuff, and haul it out of here! Stop making My Father's house a place for your own profit!

¹⁷*The disciples were astounded,* but they remembered that the Hebrew Scriptures said, "Jealous devotion for God's house consumes me."* ¹⁸Some of the Jews cried out to Him *in unison.*

Jews: Who gave You the right to shut us down? *If it is God, then* show us a sign.

Jesus: ¹⁹*You want a sign? Here it is.* Destroy this temple, and I will rebuild it in 3 days.

Jews: ²⁰*Three days?* This temple took more than 46 years to complete. You think You can replicate that feat in 3 days?

²¹The true temple was His body. ²²His disciples remembered this bold prediction after He was resurrected. *Because of this knowledge,* their faith in the Hebrew Scriptures and in Jesus' teachings grew.
²³During the Passover feast in Jerusalem, *the crowds were watching Jesus closely*; and many began to believe in Him because of the signs He was doing. ²⁴⁻²⁵But Jesus saw through to the heart of humankind, and He chose not to give them what they requested. He didn't need anyone to prove to Him the

* 2:6 Literally, two to three measures   * 2:17 Psalm 69:9

character of humanity. He knew what man was made of.

3 Nicodemus was one of the Pharisees, a man with some clout among his people. ²He came to Jesus under the cloak of darkness to question Him.

Nicodemus: Teacher, some of us have been talking. You are obviously a teacher who has come from God. The signs You are doing are proof that God is with You.

At this time, Israel's Roman occupiers have given a small group of Sadducees and Pharisees limited powers to rule, and Nicodemus is one of the Pharisees. He holds a seat on the ruling council known as the Sanhedrin, and surprisingly Nicodemus is among those who seek Jesus for His teaching. It appears that he believes more about Jesus than he wants others to know, so he comes at night.

Jesus: ³I tell you the truth: only someone who experiences birth for a second time* can *hope to* see the kingdom of God.

Nicodemus: ⁴*I am a grown man.* How can someone be born again when he is old *like me*? Am I to crawl back into my mother's womb for a second birth? *That's impossible!*

Jesus: ⁵I tell you the truth, if someone does not experience water and Spirit birth, there's no chance he will make it into God's kingdom. ⁶*Like from like.* Whatever is born from flesh is flesh; whatever is born from Spirit is spirit. ⁷Don't be shocked by My words, *but I tell you the truth.* Even you, *an educated and respected man among your people,* must be reborn *by the Spirit to enter the kingdom of God.* ⁸The wind* blows all around us as if it has a will of its own; we *feel and* hear it, but we do not understand where it has come from or where it will end up. Life in the Spirit is as if it were the wind of God.

Nicodemus: ⁹I still do not understand how this can be.

Jesus: ¹⁰Your responsibility is to instruct Israel *in matters of faith,* but you do not comprehend *the necessity of life in the Spirit?* ¹¹I tell you the truth: we speak about the things we know, and we give evidence about the things we have seen, and you choose to reject *the truth of* our witness. ¹²If you do not believe when I talk to you about ordinary, earthly realities, then heavenly realities will certainly elude you. ¹³No one has ever journeyed to heaven above except the One who has come down from heaven—the Son of Man, who is of heaven. ¹⁴Moses lifted up the serpent in the wilderness. In the same way, the Son of Man must be lifted up; ¹⁵then all those who believe in Him will experience everlasting life.

¹⁶For God expressed His love for the world in this way: He gave His only Son so that whoever believes in Him will not face everlasting destruction, but will have everlasting life. ¹⁷Here's the point. God didn't send His Son into the world to judge it; instead, He is here to rescue a world *headed toward certain destruction.*

¹⁸No one who believes in Him has to fear condemnation, yet condemnation is already the reality for everyone who refuses to believe because they reject the name of the only Son of God. ¹⁹Why does God allow for judgment *and condemnation*? Because the Light, *sent from God,* pierced through the world's darkness *to expose ill motives, hatred, gossip, greed, violence, and the like.* Still some people preferred the darkness over the light because their actions were dark. ²⁰Some of humankind hated the light. They *scampered hurriedly* back into the darkness where vices thrive and wickedness flourishes. ²¹Those who *abandon deceit and* embrace what is true, they will enter into the light where it will be clear that all their deeds come from God.

Jesus makes the point clear: stay connected to Him, and have no reason to fear. Jesus doesn't mean that at the instant someone has faith, fear simply vanishes or only good things happen in that person's life. In fact, the blessings that come with eternal life often

---

* 3:3 Or "from above"   * 3:8 "Wind" and "spirit" are the same word in Greek.

have nothing to do with present or future circumstances, but they have everything to do with the individual's connections to God and others. That is John's message to his listeners. God came to earth embodied in flesh, and then He reached His greatest acclaim through a torturous death. If this is all true, then believers will find strength and beauty in places never imagined. Abiding in Jesus the Anointed is the good life, regardless of the external circumstances.

---

²²Not long after, Jesus and His disciples traveled to the Judean countryside where they could enjoy one another's company and ritually cleanse *new followers* through baptism.* ²³⁻²⁴About the same time, *Jesus' cousin* John—*the wandering prophet* who had not yet been imprisoned—was *upriver* at Aenon near Salim baptizing *scores of* people in the abundant waters there. ²⁵John's activities raised questions about the nature of purification among his followers and a religious leader, ²⁶so they approached him with their questions.

John's Followers: Teacher, the One who was with you *earlier* on the other side of the Jordan, the One whom you have been pointing to, is baptizing* the multitudes who are coming to Him.

John the Baptist: ²⁷Apart from the gifts that come from heaven, no one can receive anything at all. ²⁸I have said it many times, and you have heard me—I am not the Anointed One; I am the one who comes before Him. ²⁹If you are confused, consider this: the groom is the one with the bride. The best man takes his place close by and listens for him. When he hears the voice of the groom, he is swept up in the joy *of the moment*. So hear me. My joy could not be more complete. ³⁰He, *the groom,* must take center stage; and I, *the best man,* must step to His side.

³¹If someone comes from heaven above, he ranks above it all *and speaks of heavenly things*. If someone comes from earth, he speaks of earthly things. The One from the heavens is superior; He is over all. ³²He reveals the mysteries seen and *realities* heard *of the heavens above,* but no one below is listening. ³³Those who are listening and accept His witness *to these truths* have gone on record. They acknowledge the fact that God is true! ³⁴The One sent from God speaks with the very words of God and abounds with the very Spirit and essence of God. ³⁵The Father loves the Son and withholds nothing from Him. ³⁶Those who believe in the Son will bask in eternal life, but those who disobey the Son will never experience life. They will know only God's lingering wrath.

4 The picture was becoming clear to the Pharisees that Jesus had gained a following much larger than that of John the Baptist, *the wandering prophet*. Now He could see *that the Pharisees were beginning to plot against Him*. ²This was because His disciples were busy ritually cleansing many new disciples through baptism,* ³He chose to leave Judea *where most Pharisees lived* and return to *a safer location in* Galilee. ⁴This was a trip that would take them through Samaria.

For Jews in Israel, Samaria is a place to be avoided. Before Solomon's death 1,000 years earlier, the regions of Samaria and Judea were part of a united Israel. After the rebellion that divided the kingdom, Samaria became a hotbed of idol worship. The northern kings made alliances that corrupted the people by introducing foreign customs and strange gods. They even had the nerve to build a temple to the True God on Mt. Gerizim to rival the one in Jerusalem. By the time the twelve are traveling with Jesus, it has long been evident that the Samaritans have lost their way. By marrying outsiders, they have polluted the land. Israel's Jews consider them to be half-breeds—mongrels—and the Jews know to watch out for them or else be bitten by temptation.

---

* 3:22 Literally, immerse, to show repentance   * 3:26 Literally, immersing, to show repentance   * 4:2 Literally, immersing, to show repentance

5-8In a *small* Samaritan town known as Sychar, Jesus *and His entourage* stopped to rest at the historic well that Jacob gave his son Joseph. It was about noon when Jesus found a spot to sit close to the well while the disciples ventured off to find provisions. *From His vantage, He watched as* a Samaritan woman approached to draw some water. *Unexpectedly* He spoke to her.

Jesus: Would you *draw water, and* give Me a drink?

Woman: 9I cannot believe that You, a Jew, would associate with me, a Samaritan woman; much less ask me to give You a drink.

Jews, you see, have no dealings with Samaritans.

Also, a man never approaches a woman like this in public. Jesus is breaking accepted social barriers with this confrontation.

Jesus: 10You don't know the gift of God or who is asking you for a drink *of this water from Jacob's well.* Because if you did, you would have asked Him *for something greater;* and He would have given you the living water.

Woman: 11Sir, You sit by this deep well *a thirsty man* without a bucket in sight. Where does this living water come from? 12Are You claiming superiority to our father Jacob who labored long and hard to dig *and maintain* this well so that he could share clean water with his sons, *grandchildren,* and cattle?

Jesus: 13Drink this water, and your thirst is quenched only for a moment. *You must return to this well again and again.* 14I offer water that will become a wellspring within you that gives life throughout eternity. You will never be thirsty again.

Woman: 15*Please*, Sir, give me some of this water, so I'll never be thirsty and never again have to make the trip to this well.

Jesus: 16Then bring your husband to Me.

Woman: 17-18I do not have a husband.

Jesus: Technically you are telling the truth. But you have had five husbands and are currently living with a man you are not married to.

Woman: 19Sir, it is obvious to me that You are a prophet. 20Our fathers worshiped here on this mountain, but Your people say that Jerusalem is the only place for all to worship. *Which is it?*

Jesus: 21-24Woman, I tell you that neither *is so*. Believe this: a new day is coming—in fact, it's already here—when the importance will not be placed on the time and place of worship but on the truthful hearts of worshipers. You worship what you don't know while we worship what we do know, for God's salvation is coming through the Jews. The Father is spirit, and He is seeking followers whose worship is sourced in truth and deeply spiritual as well. Regardless of whether you are in Jerusalem or on this mountain, if you do not seek the Father, then you do not worship.

Woman: 25These mysteries will be made clear by He who is promised, the Anointed One.

Jesus: 26The Anointed is speaking to you. I am the One you have been looking for.

27The disciples returned to Him *and gathered around Him* in amazement that He would *openly break their customs by* speaking to this woman, but none of them would ask Him what He was looking for or why He was speaking with her. 28The woman went back to the town, leaving her water pot behind. She stopped men and women on the streets and told them about what had happened.

Woman: 29I met a stranger who knew everything about me. Come and see for yourselves; can He be the Anointed One?

30A crowd came out of the city and approached Jesus. 31During all of this, the disciples were urging Jesus to eat the food they gathered.

Jesus: 32I have food to eat that you know nothing about.

Disciples (to one another): 33Is it possible someone else has brought Him food while we were away?

Jesus: [34]I receive My nourishment by serving the will of the Father who sent Me and completing His work. [35]You have heard others say, *"Be patient; we have four more months to wait until the crops are ready for the harvest."* I say, take a closer look and you will see that the fields are ripe and ready for the harvest. [36]The harvester is collecting his pay, harvesting fruit ripe for eternal life. So even now, he and the sower are celebrating *their fortune.* [37]The saying *may be old, but it* is true: "One person sows, and another reaps." [38]I sent you to harvest where you have not labored; someone else took the time to plant and cultivate, and you feast on the fruit of their labor.

[39]Meanwhile, because one woman shared with her neighbors how Jesus exposed her past and present, the village *of Sychar* was transformed—many Samaritans heard and believed. [40]The Samaritans approached Jesus and repeatedly invited Him to stay with them, so He lingered there for two days *on their account.* [41]With the words that came from His mouth, there were many more believing Samaritans. [42]They began their faith journey because of the testimony of the woman *beside the well;* but when they heard for themselves, they were convinced the One they were hearing was and is God's Anointed, *the Liberating King,* sent to rescue the entire world.

[43-45]After two days *of teaching and conversation,* Jesus proceeded to Galilee where His countrymen received Him *with familiar smiles.* After all, they witnessed His miracle at the feast in Jerusalem; but Jesus understood and often quoted *the maxim:* "No one honors a hometown prophet."

These old friends should be the first to believe, but it takes outsiders like the Samaritans to recognize Him.

[46-47]As Jesus traveled to Cana (the village in Galilee where He transformed the water into *fine* wine), He was met by a government official. This man had heard *a rumor that* Jesus had left Judea and was heading to Galilee, and he came *in desperation* begging for Jesus' help because his young son was near death. *He was fearful that unless* Jesus would go with him to Capernaum, his son would have no hope.

Jesus *(to the official):* [48]*My word is not enough*; you only believe when you see miraculous signs.

Official: [49]Sir, this is my son; please come with me before he dies.

Jesus *(interrupting him):* [50]Go home. Your son will live.

When he heard the voice of Jesus, faith took hold of him and he turned to go home. [51]Before he reached his village, his servants met him on the road celebrating his son's miraculous recovery.

Official: [52]What time did this happen?

Servants: Yesterday about one o'clock in the afternoon.

[53]At that moment, it dawned on the father the exact time that Jesus spoke the words, "He will live." After that, he believed; and *when he told* his family *about his amazing encounter with this Jesus,* they believed too. [54]This was the second sign Jesus performed when He came back to Galilee from Judea.

5 When these events were completed, Jesus led His followers to Jerusalem where they would celebrate a Jewish feast* together.

Jesus takes His disciples into one of the most miserable places they have ever seen. The suffering and impurity is frightening, but He comes to serve these precious people.

[2-3]In Jerusalem they came upon a pool by the sheep gate surrounded by five covered porches. In Hebrew this place is called Bethesda.

Crowds of people lined the area, lying around the porches. All of these people were *disabled in some way;* some were blind, lame, paralyzed, or plagued by diseases[; and they were waiting for the waters to move. [4]From time to time, a heavenly messenger would come to stir the water in the pool. Whoever reached the water first and got in after it was agitated would be healed of his or her disease].* [5-6]In the crowd, Jesus noticed one particular man who had been living with his

---

* 5:1 Perhaps Passover   * 5:4 Some early manuscripts omit the end of verse 3 and all of verse 4.

disability for 38 years. He knew this man had been waiting here a long time.

Jesus (*to the disabled man*): Are you *here in this place* hoping to be healed?

Disabled Man: [7]Kind Sir, I wait, *like all of these people,* for the waters to stir; *but I cannot walk. If I am to be healed in the waters,* someone must carry me into the pool. Without a helping hand, someone else beats me to the water's edge each time it is stirred.

Jesus: [8]Stand up, carry your mat, and walk.

[9]At the moment Jesus uttered these words, a healing energy coursed through the man and returned life to his limbs—he stood and walked *for the first time in 38 years.* But this was the Sabbath Day; *and any work, including carrying a mat, was prohibited on this day.*

It is impossible to imagine this man's excitement. His entire life has been defined by his illness. Now he is free from it. Free from the pain and weakness. Free from the depression that gripped his soul. Free, too, from the shame he always knew. Now he does not just walk—he runs and celebrates with friends and family. Everyone is rejoicing with him, except for some of the Jewish leaders. Instead, they drill him with questions as if they can disregard this miracle.

Jewish Leaders (*to the man who had been healed*): [10]Must you be reminded that it is the Sabbath? You are not allowed to carry your mat today!

Formerly Disabled Man: [11]The man who healed me gave me specific instructions to carry my mat and go.

Jewish Leaders: [12]Who is the man who gave you these instructions? *How can we identify Him?*

[13]The man genuinely did not know who it was that healed him. In the midst of the crowd *and the excitement of his renewed*

health, Jesus had slipped away. [14]Some time later, Jesus found him in the temple and again spoke to him.

Jesus: Take a look at your body; it has been made whole and strong. So avoid a life of sin, or else a calamity greater than any disability may befall you.

[15]The man went immediately to tell the Jewish leaders that Jesus was the mysterious healer. [16]So they began pursuing and attacking Jesus because He performed these miracles on the Sabbath.

Jesus (*to His attackers*): [17]My Father is at work. So I, too, am working.

This issue keeps arising from the Jewish leaders. They do not appreciate the good things Jesus does on the Sabbath. Most Jews cower at the rebuke from these men, but Jesus does not. He is very clear about this. He cares for the poor, the sick, and the marginalized more than He cares for how some people may interpret and apply God's law. It is easy to follow a set of rules; it is much harder to care for the things of the heart. He also makes it clear that those who follow His path are put on earth to serve. His followers' service comes out of love for Him. All who follow Him are to love and to serve, especially on the Sabbath.

[18]He was justifying the importance of His work on the Sabbath, claiming God as His Father in ways that suggested He was equal to God. These pious religious leaders sought an opportunity to kill Jesus, and these words fueled their hatred.

Jesus: [19]The truth is that the Son does nothing on His own; *all these actions are led by the Father.* The Son watches the Father closely and then mimics the work of the Father. [20]The Father loves the Son, so He does not hide His actions. Instead, He shows Him everything, and the things not yet revealed by the Father will dumbfound you. [21]The Father can give life to those who are dead; in the same way, the Son can give the gift of life to those He chooses.

²²The Father does not *exert His power to* judge anyone. Instead, He has given the authority as Judge to the Son. ²³So all of creation will honor *and worship* the Son as they do the Father. If you do not honor the Son, then you dishonor the Father who sent Him.

²⁴I tell you the truth: eternal life belongs to those who hear My voice and believe in the One who sent Me. These people have no reason to fear judgment because they have already left death and entered life.

²⁵I tell you the truth: a new day is imminent—in fact, it has arrived—when the voice of the Son of God will penetrate death's domain, and everyone who hears will live. ²⁶⁻²⁷You see, the Father radiates with life; and He also animates the Son *of God* with the same life-giving *beauty and* power to exercise judgment *over all of creation.* Indeed, the Son of God is also the Son of Man. ²⁸If this sounds amazing to you, what is even more amazing is that when the time comes, those buried long ago will hear His voice *through all the rocks, sod, and soil* ²⁹and step out *of decay into resurrection. When this hour arrives,* those who did good will be resurrected to life, and those who did evil will be resurrected to judgment.

³⁰I have not ever acted, and will not in the future act, on My own. I listen *to the directions of the One who sent Me* and act *on these divine instructions. For this reason,* My judgment is always fair and never self-serving. I'm committed to pursuing God's agenda and not My own.

³¹If I stand as the lone witness to My true identity, then I can be dismissed as a liar. ³²*But if you listen,* you will hear another testify about Me, and I know what He says about Me is genuine and true. ³³You sent *messengers* to John, and he told the truth *to everyone who would listen.* ³⁴Still his message about Me *originated in heaven,* not in mortal man. I am telling you these things *for one reason*—so that you might be rescued. ³⁵*The voice of* John the Baptist, *the wandering prophet,* is like a light in the darkness; and for a time, you took great joy and pleasure in the light he offered.

³⁶There's another witness standing in My corner who is greater than John *or any other man.* The mission that brings Me here, and the things I am called to do, demonstrate the authenticity of My calling which comes directly from the Father. ³⁷In the act of sending Me, the Father has endorsed Me. *None of you really knows the Father.* You have never heard His voice or seen His profile. ³⁸His word does not abide in you because you do not believe in the One sent by the Father.

³⁹Here you are scouring through the Scriptures, hoping that you will find eternal life among a pile of scrolls. *What you don't seem to understand is that* the Scriptures point to Me. ⁴⁰*Here I am with you,* and still you reject the truth *contained in the law and prophets* by refusing to come to Me so that you can have life.

Jesus is the source of life, the animating energy of creation that humanity desperately lacks.

⁴¹This kind of glory does not come from mortal men. ⁴²And I see that you do not possess the love of God. ⁴³I have *pursued you,* coming here in My Father's name, and you have turned Me away. If someone else were to approach you with a different set of credentials, you would welcome him. ⁴⁴*That's why it is hard to see* how true faith is even possible for you: you are consumed by the approval of other men, *longing to look good in their eyes;* and yet you disregard the approval of the one true God. ⁴⁵Don't worry that I might bring you up on charges before My Father. Moses is your accuser even though you've put your hope in him ⁴⁶because if you believed *what* Moses had to *say,* then you would believe in Me because he wrote about Me. ⁴⁷But if you ignore Moses and the deeper meaning of his writings, then how will you ever believe what I have to say?

6 Once this had transpired, Jesus made His way to the other side of the Sea of Galilee (which some these days call the Sea of Tiberias). ²As Jesus walked, a large crowd pursued Him hoping to see new signs *and miracles;* His healings of the sick and lame were garnering great attention. ³Jesus went up a mountain and found a place to sit down *and teach.* His disciples gathered around. ⁴The celebration of the Passover, one of the principal Jewish feasts, would take place soon. ⁵But when Jesus looked up, He

could see an immense crowd coming toward Him. Jesus approached Philip.

Jesus *(to Philip)*: Where is a place to buy bread so these people may eat?

[6]Jesus knew what He was planning to do, but He asked Philip nonetheless. He had something to teach, and it started with a test.

Philip: [7]I could work for more than half of a year* and still not have the money to buy enough bread to give each person a very small piece.

[8]Andrew, the disciple who was Simon Peter's brother, spoke up.

Andrew: [9]I met a young boy in the crowd carrying five barley loaves and two fish, but that is practically useless in feeding a crowd this large.

Jesus: [10]Tell the people to sit down.

They all sat together on a large grassy area. *Those counting the people reported* approximately 5,000 men—*not including the women and children*—sitting in the crowd. [11]Jesus picked up the bread, gave thanks to God, and passed it to everyone. He repeated this ritual with the fish. *Men, women, and children* all ate until their hearts were content. [12]When the people had all they could eat, He told the disciples *to gather the leftovers.*

Jesus: Go and collect the leftovers, so we are not wasteful.

[13]They filled 12 baskets with fragments of the five barley loaves. [14]After witnessing this sign that Jesus did, the people stirred in conversation.

Crowd: This man must be the Prophet *God said was* coming into the world.

[15]Jesus sensed the people were planning to mount a revolution *against Israel's Roman occupiers* and make Him king, so He withdrew farther up the mountain by Himself.

another in their land. As conquerors go, the Romans aren't all that bad. They allow the Jews to worship God in His temple, and they appoint some of them to government positions. Of course, the Judeans still long to rule themselves and throw the Roman rulers out. Some think Jesus is just the man to lead that revolution. But political upheaval isn't what He is teaching, and it isn't why He has come to earth.

[16]Later that evening the disciples walked down to the sea, [17]boarded a boat, and set sail toward Capernaum. Twilight gave way to darkness. Jesus had not yet joined them. [18]*Suddenly,* the waves rose and a fierce wind began *to rock the boat.* [19]After rowing three or four miles* *through the stormy seas,* they spotted Jesus approaching the boat walking mysteriously upon the deep waters that surrounded them. They panicked.

Jesus *(to the disciples)*: [20]I am the One. Don't be afraid.

[21]They welcomed Jesus aboard their small vessel; and when He stepped into the boat, the next thing they knew, they were ashore at their destination.

[22]The following day some people gathered on the other side of the sea and saw that only one boat had been there; *they were perplexed.* They remembered seeing the disciples getting into the boat without Jesus.

[23]Other boats were arriving from Tiberias near the grassy area where the Lord offered thanks and passed out bread. [24]When this crowd could not find Him or His disciples, they boarded their small boats and crossed the sea to Capernaum looking for Him. [25]When they found Jesus across the sea, they questioned Him.

Crowd: Teacher, when did You arrive at Capernaum?

Jesus: [26]I tell you the truth—you are tracking Me down because I fed you, not because you saw signs from God. [27]Don't spend your life chasing food that spoils and rots.

* 6:7 Literally, 200 denarii   * 6:19 Literally, 25 or 30 stadia

Instead, seek the food that lasts into all the ages and comes from the Son of Man, the One on whom God the Father has placed His seal.

Crowd: 28What do we have to do to accomplish the Father's works?

Jesus: 29If you want to do God's work, then believe in the One He sent.

Crowd: 30Can You show us a miraculous sign? *Something spectacular?* If we see something like that, it will help us to believe. 31Our fathers ate manna when they wandered in the desert. The Hebrew Scriptures say, "He gave them bread from heaven to eat."*

Jesus: 32I tell you the truth: Moses did not give you bread from heaven; it is My Father who offers you true bread from heaven. 33The bread of God comes down out of heaven and breathes life into the cosmos.

Crowd: 34Master, we want a boundless supply of this bread.

Jesus: 35I am the bread that gives life. If you come to My table and eat, you will never go hungry. Believe in Me, and you will never go thirsty. 36Here I am standing in front of you, and still you don't believe. 37All that My Father gives to Me comes to Me. I will receive everyone; I will not send away anyone who comes to Me. 38And here's the reason: I have come down from heaven not to pursue My own agenda but to do what He desires. I am here on behalf of the Father who sent Me. 39He sent Me to care for all He has given Me so that nothing *and no one* will perish. *In the end,* on the last day, He wants everything to be resurrected *into new life.* 40So if you want to know the will of the Father, know this: everyone who sees the Son and believes in Him will live eternally; and on the last day, I am the One who will resurrect him.

41Some of the Jews began to grumble *quietly* against Him because He said, "I am the bread that came down from heaven."

Crowd: 42Isn't Jesus the son of Joseph? We know His parents! *We know where He came from,* so how can He claim to have "come down from heaven"?

Jesus: 43Stop grumbling *under your breaths.* 44If the Father who sent Me does not draw you, then there's no way you can come to Me. But I will resurrect everyone who does come on the last day. 45Among the prophets, it's written, "Everyone will be taught of God."* So everyone who has heard and learned from the Father finds Me. 46No one has seen the Father, except the One sent from God. He has seen the Father. 47I am telling you the truth: the one who accepts these things has eternal life. 48I am the bread that gives life. 49Your fathers ate manna in the wilderness, and they died *as you know.* 50But there is another bread that comes from heaven; if you eat this bread, you will not die. 51I am the living bread that has come down from heaven *to rescue those who eat it.* Anyone who eats this bread will live forever. The bread that I will give breathes life into the cosmos. This bread is My flesh.

52*The low whispers of* some of Jesus' detractors turned into an out-and-out debate.

Crowd: *What is He talking about?* How is He able to give us His flesh to eat?

Jesus: 53I tell you the truth; unless you eat the flesh of the Son of Man and drink His blood, you will not know life. 54If you eat My flesh and drink My blood, then you will have eternal life and I will raise you up at the end of time. 55My flesh and blood provide true nourishment. 56If you eat My flesh and drink My blood, you will abide in Me and I will abide in you. 57The Father of life who sent Me has given life to Me; and as you eat My flesh, I will give life to you. 58This is bread that came down from heaven; I am not like the manna that your fathers ate and then died! If you eat this bread, your life will never end.

59He spoke these words in the synagogue as part of His teaching mission in Capernaum. 60Many disciples heard what He said, and they had questions *of their own.*

Disciples: How are we supposed to understand all of this? It is a hard teaching.

61Jesus was aware that even His disciples were murmuring about this.

* 6:31 Exodus 16:4   * 6:45 Isaiah 54:13

How is it possible to follow this path and believe these truths? To be honest, it is not easy. In fact, some find this so hard that they leave Jesus for good. The rest readily admit they are still working on what it means to follow Him. So Jesus leaves behind a number of practices to help believers. One of these is known as the Lord's Supper. Jesus instructs His disciples to break bread and share wine to remember how He will allow His body to be broken for all humankind. In some beautiful, mysterious way, Jesus is present in the simple elements of bread and wine, so the worshiper may touch Him, taste His richness, and remember His most glorious hours on the cross. In that moment, He embraces all darkness and shame and transforms them into light. As believers come to the table together and feast on His light, life seems more hopeful and complete. Taking the bread and the wine means affirming the reality that the One who has come to liberate souls is among and within His people.

Jesus: Has My teaching offended you? ⁶²What if you were to see the Son of Man ascend *to return* to where He came from? ⁶³The Spirit brings life. The flesh has nothing to offer. The words I have been teaching you are spirit and life, ⁶⁴but some of you do not believe.

From the first day *Jesus began to call disciples,* He knew those who did not have genuine faith. He knew, too, who would betray Him.

Jesus: ⁶⁵This is why I have been telling you that no one comes to Me without the Father's blessing and guidance.

⁶⁶After hearing these teachings, many of His disciples walked away and no longer followed Jesus.

Jesus *(to the twelve)*: ⁶⁷Do you want to walk away too?

Simon Peter: ⁶⁸Lord, if we were to go, whom would we follow? You speak the words that give everlasting life. ⁶⁹We believe and recognize that You are the Holy One sent by God.*

Jesus: ⁷⁰I chose each one of you, the twelve, Myself. But one of you is a devil.

⁷¹This cryptic comment referred to Judas, the son of Simon Iscariot, for he was the one of the twelve who was going to betray Him.

7 After these events, *it was time for Jesus to move on.* He began a long walk through the Galilean countryside. He was purposefully avoiding Judea because

of *the violent threats made against Him by* the Jews there who wanted to kill Him. ²*It was fall,* the time of year when the Jews celebrated the Festival of Booths.

On this holiday, everyone camps in temporary quarters, called booths, to remember that God was with their ancestors when they wandered for 40 years without a home.

Brothers of Jesus *(to Jesus)*: ³Let's get out of here and go *south* to Judea so You can show Your disciples there what You are capable of doing. ⁴No one who seeks the public eye is content to work in secret. If You want to perform these signs, then step forward on the world's stage; *don't hide up here in the hills, Jesus.*

⁵Jesus' own brothers *were speaking contemptuously;* they did not yet believe in Him, *just as the people in His hometown did not see Him as anything more than Joseph's son.*

Jesus: ⁶My time has not yet arrived; but for you My brothers, *by all means,* it is always the right time. ⁷*You have nothing to worry about because* the world doesn't hate you, but it despises Me because I am always exposing the dark evil in its works. ⁸Go on to the feast without Me; I am not going *right now* because My time is not yet at hand.

⁹This conversation came to an *abrupt* end, and Jesus stayed in Galilee ¹⁰until His brothers were gone. Then He, too, went up to Jerusalem. But He traveled in secret to avoid

* 6:69 Other ancient manuscripts read, "You are God's Anointed, *the Liberating King, the Son of the Living God.*"

drawing any public attention. ¹¹Some Jewish leaders were searching for Him at the feast and asking the crowds where they could find Him. ¹²The crowds would talk in groups: some favored Jesus and thought He was a good man; others disliked Him and thought He was leading people astray. ¹³*All of these conversations took place in whispers.* No one was willing to speak openly about Jesus for fear of the religious leaders.

¹⁴In the middle of the festival, Jesus marched directly into the temple and started to teach. ¹⁵Some of the Jews *who heard Him* were amazed at Jesus' ability, and people questioned repeatedly:

Jews: How can this man be so wise *about the Hebrew Scriptures*? He has never had a formal education.

Jesus: ¹⁶I do not claim ownership of My words; they are *a gift* from the One who sent Me. ¹⁷If anyone is willing to act according to His purposes *and is open to hearing truth*, he will know the source of My teaching. Does it come from God or from Me? ¹⁸If a man speaks his own words, *constantly quoting himself*, he is after adulation. But I chase only after glory for the One who sent Me. My intention is *authentic and* true. You'll find no wrong *motives* in Me.

¹⁹Moses gave you the law, didn't he? Then how can you *blatantly* ignore the law and look for an opportunity to murder Me?

Notice how Jesus changes in tone and subject. This shift seems abrupt because the Pharisees' plotting is yet to be exposed.

Crowd: ²⁰You must be possessed with a demon! Who is trying to kill You?

Jesus: ²¹*Listen*, all it took was for Me to do one thing, *heal a crippled man*, and you all were astonished. ²²Don't you remember how Moses passed down circumcision as a tradition of our ancestors? When you pick up a knife to circumcise on the Sabbath, *isn't that work*? ²³If a male is circumcised on the Sabbath to keep the law of Moses intact, how can making one man whole on the Sabbath be a cause for your violent rage? ²⁴You should not judge by outward appearance. When you judge, search for what is right and just.

Some People of Jerusalem: ²⁵There is the man they are seeking to kill; surely He must be the one. ²⁶But here He is, speaking out in the open to the crowd, while they have not spoken a word to *stop or challenge* Him. Do these leaders now believe He is the Anointed One? ²⁷But He can't be; we know where this man comes from, but the true origin of the Anointed will be a mystery to all of us.

Jesus (*speaking aloud as He teaches on the temple's porch*): ²⁸*You think* you know Me and where I have come from, but I have not come here on My own. I have been sent by the One who embodies truth. You do not know Him. ²⁹I know Him because I came from Him. He has sent Me.

³⁰Some were trying to seize Him because of His words, but no one laid as much as a finger on Him—His time had not yet arrived. ³¹In the crowd, there were many in whom faith was taking hold.

Believers in the Crowd: When the Anointed arrives, will He perform any more signs than this man has done?

³²Some Pharisees *were hanging back in the crowd*, overhearing the gossip about Him. The temple authorities and the Pharisees *took action and* sent officers to arrest Jesus.

Jesus: ³³I am going to be with you for a little while longer; then I will return to the One who sent Me. ³⁴You will look for Me, but you will not be able to find Me. Where I am, you are unable to come.

Some Jews in the Crowd (*to each other*): ³⁵Where could He possibly go that we could not find Him? You don't think He's about to go into the Dispersion* and teach our people scattered among the Greeks, do you? ³⁶What do you think He means, "You will look for Me, but you will not be able to find Me," and, "Where I am, you are unable to come"?

³⁷On the last day, the biggest day of the festival, Jesus stood again and spoke aloud.

Jesus: If any of you is thirsty, come to Me and drink. ³⁸If you believe in Me, the

---

* 7:35 Literally, the Diaspora (Greek for "scattering"). The Diaspora refers to those Jews who were exiled or settled outside the traditional lands of Israel.

Hebrew Scriptures say that rivers of living water will flow from within you.*

[39] Jesus was referring to *the realities of life in the Spirit made available to everyone who believes in Him.* But the Spirit had not yet arrived because Jesus had not been glorified.

V

The Holy Spirit connects believers to the Father and His Son. So any fear about being disconnected from God may be abandoned; the Creator of the Universe dwells within His people, sustains them, and will accomplish the impossible through them.

Some of the Crowd: [40] This man is definitely the Prophet.

Others: [41] This is God's Anointed, *the Liberating King!*

Still Others: Is it possible for the Anointed to come from Galilee? [42] Don't the Hebrew Scriptures say that He will come from Bethlehem,* King David's village, and be a descendant of King David?

[43] *Rumors and* opinions about the true identity of Jesus divided the crowd. [44] Some wanted to arrest Him, but no one dared to touch Him.

[45] The officers *who had been sent by* the chief priests and Pharisees *to take Jesus into custody* returned *empty-handed,* and they faced some hard questions.

Chief Priest and Pharisees: *Where is Jesus?* Why didn't you capture Him?

Officers: [46] *We listened to Him.* Never has a man spoken like this man.

Pharisees: [47] So you have also been led astray? [48] Can you find one leader or educated Pharisee who believes this man? *Of course not.* [49] This crowd is plagued by ignorance about the teachings of the law; *that is why they will listen to Him.* That is also why they are under God's curse.

[50] Nicodemus, *the Pharisee* who approached Jesus *under the cloak of darkness,* was present when the officers returned empty-handed. He addressed the leaders.

Nicodemus: [51] Does our law condemn someone without first giving him a fair hearing and learning something about him?

Pharisees *(ignoring Nicodemus's legal point):* [52] Are you from Galilee too? Look it up for yourself; no real prophet is supposed to come from Galilee.

[[53] The time came for everyone to go home.

8 Jesus went to the Mount of Olives. [2] He awoke early in the morning to return to the temple. *When He arrived,* the people surrounded Him, so He sat down and began to teach them. [3] *While He was teaching,* the scribes and Pharisees brought in a woman who was caught in the act of adultery; and they stood her before Jesus.

Pharisees: [4] Teacher, this woman was caught in the act of adultery. [5] Moses says in the law that we are to kill such women by stoning. What do You say about it?

[6] This was all set up as a test for Jesus; His answers would give them grounds to accuse Him *of crimes against Moses' law.* Jesus bent over and wrote something in the dirt with His finger. [7] They persisted in badgering Jesus, so He stood up straight.

Jesus: Let the first stone be thrown by the one among you who has not sinned.

[8] Once again Jesus bent down to the ground and resumed writing with His finger. [9] The Pharisees who heard Him *stood still for a few moments and then* began to leave slowly, one by one, beginning with the older men. Eventually only Jesus and the woman remained, [10] and Jesus looked up.

Jesus: *Dear* woman, where is everyone? *Are we alone?* Did no one step forward to condemn you?

Woman Caught in Adultery: [11] Lord, no one *has condemned me.*

---

* 7:38 Isaiah 44:3; 55:1; 58:11   * 7:42 Micah 5:1-2

Jesus: Well, I do not condemn you either; *all I ask is that you* go and from now on avoid the sins that plague you.]*

¹²*On another occasion,* Jesus spoke to the crowds again.

Jesus: I am the light that shines through the cosmos; if you walk with Me, you will thrive in the *nourishing* light that gives life and will not know darkness.

Pharisees: ¹³Jesus, what You are claiming about Yourself cannot possibly be true. The only person bearing witness is You.

Jesus: ¹⁴Even if I am making *bold* claims about Myself—*who I am, what I have come to do*—I am speaking the truth. You see, I know where I came from and where I will go *when I am done here.* You know neither where I come from nor where I will go. ¹⁵You spend your time judging *by the wrong criteria,* by human standards; but I am not here to judge anyone. ¹⁶If I were to judge, then My judgment would be based on truth; but I would not judge anyone alone. I act in harmony with the One who sent Me. ¹⁷Your law states that if the testimonies of two witnesses agree, their testimony is true. ¹⁸Well, I testify about Myself, and so does the Father who sent Me here.

Pharisees: ¹⁹Where is the Father *who testifies on Your behalf?*

Jesus: You don't know the Father or Me. If you knew Me, then you would also know the Father.

²⁰Jesus said all of these things in the treasury while He was teaching in the temple; *followers and opponents alike gathered to hear Him,* but none of His enemies tried to seize Him because His time had not yet come.

Jesus *(to the crowds):* ²¹I am leaving this place, and you will look for Me and die in your sin. For where I am going, you are unable to come.

Jews: ²²Is He suicidal? He keeps saying, "Where I am going, you are unable to come."

Jesus: ²³You originate from *the earth* below, and I have come from *the heavens* above. You are from this world, and I am not.

²⁴That's why I told you that you will die here as a result of your sins. Unless you believe I am who I have said I am, your sins will lead to your death.

Jews: ²⁵Who exactly are You?

Jesus: From the beginning of My mission, I have been telling you who I am. ²⁶I have so much to say about you, so many judgments to render; *but if you hear one thing,* hear that the One who sent Me is true, and all the things I have heard from Him I speak into the world.

²⁷The people had not understood that Jesus was teaching about the Father.

Jesus: ²⁸Whenever *the day comes and* you lift up the Son of Man, then you will know that I am He. *It will be clear then* that I am not acting alone, but that I am speaking the things I have learned directly from the Father. ²⁹The One who sent Me is with Me; He has not abandoned Me because I always do what pleases Him.

³⁰As Jesus was speaking, many in the crowd believed in Him.

Even though many believe, they cannot imagine what He means about the lifting up of the Son of Man.

Jesus *(to the new Jewish believers):* ³¹If you *hear My voice and* abide in My word, you are truly My disciples; ³²you will know the truth, and that truth will give you freedom.

Jewish Believers: ³³We are Abraham's children, and we have never been enslaved to anyone. How can You say to us, "You will be set free"?

Jesus: ³⁴I tell you the truth: everyone who commits sin surrenders his freedom to sin. He is a *slave to sin's power.* ³⁵Even a household slave does not live in the home like a member of the family, but a son belongs there forever. ³⁶So *think of it this way:* if the Son comes to make you free, you will really be free.

Jesus notices that some of His opponents are listening, so He speaks louder and turns His remarks to them.

* 7:53–8:11 Many early manuscripts omit these verses.

[37] I know you are descendants of Abraham, but here you are plotting to murder Me because you do not welcome My voice into your lives. [38] As I speak, I am painting you a picture of what I have seen with My Father; here you are repeating the things you have seen from your father.

Jews: [39] Abraham is our father.

Jesus: If you are truly Abraham's children, then act like Abraham! [40] From what I see you are trying to kill Me, a man who has told you the truth that comes from the Father. This is not something Abraham would do, [41] but you are doing what you have learned from your father.

Jews: We were not born from adulterous parents; we have one Father: God.

Jesus: [42] I come from the one True God, and I'm not here on My own. He sent Me *on a mission.* If God were your Father, you would *know that and would* love Me. [43] You don't even understand what I'm saying. *Do you?* Why not? It is because You cannot stand to hear My voice. [44] You are just like your true father, the devil; and you spend your time pursuing the things your father loves. He started out as a killer, and he cannot tolerate truth because he is void of anything true. At the core of his character, he is a liar; everything he speaks originates in these lies because he is the father of lies. [45] So when I speak truth, you don't believe Me. [46-47] If I speak the truth, why don't you believe Me? If you belong to God's family, then why can't you hear God speak? The answer is clear; you are not in God's family. *I speak truth, and you don't believe Me.* Can any of you convict Me of sin?

Jews: [48] We were right when we called You a demon-possessed Samaritan.

Jesus: [49-50] I'm not taken by demons. You dishonor Me, but I give *all glory and* honor to the Father. But I am not pursuing My own fame. There is only One who pursues and renders justice. [51] I tell you the truth, anyone who *hears My voice and* keeps My word will never experience death.

Jews: [52] We are even more confident now that You are demon-possessed. *Just go down the list:* Abraham died, the prophets all died. Yet You say, "If you keep My word, you will never taste death." [53] Are you greater than our father Abraham? He died; *remember?* Prophets—are any of them still alive? No. Who do You think You are?

Jesus: [54] If I were trying to make Myself somebody important, *it would be a waste of time.* That kind of fame is worth nothing. It is the Father who *is behind Me, urging Me on,* giving Me praise. You say, "He is our God," [55] but you are not in relationship with Him. I know Him *intimately*; even if I said anything other than the truth, I would be a liar, like you. I know Him, and I do as He says. [56] Your father Abraham anticipated the time when I would come, and he celebrated My coming.

Jews: [57] You aren't even 50 years old, yet You have seen *and talked with* Abraham?

Jesus: [58] I tell you the truth; I AM before Abraham was born.

[59] The people picked up stones to hurl at Him, but Jesus slipped out of the temple. *Their murderous rage would have to wait.*

V

John and many people in his community are Jews. As a son of Abraham, his criticism of certain Jewish leaders is not a criticism of a whole people. He's not stereotyping or making generalizations. "The Jews" he remembers in this passage are a corrupt group of power brokers who conspire against Jesus with the Romans to have Him crucified and who later have John's own followers expelled from the synagogue. Their behavior may be compared to the behavior of those Israelites condemned by Old Testament prophets. Prophets have the duty—Jeremiah said he had "a fire in his bones" (20:9)—to speak for God and condemn hypocrisy and unbelief wherever it is found, especially when it's found close to home. That's what John's doing when recalling this event.

9

While walking along the road, Jesus saw a man who was blind since his birth.

Disciples: ²Teacher, who sinned? *Who is responsible for this man's blindness?* Did he commit sins that merited this punishment? If not his sins, is it the sins of his parents?

Jesus: ³Neither. His blindness cannot be *explained or* traced to any particular person's sins. He is blind so the deeds of God may be put on display. ⁴While it is daytime, we must do the works of the One who sent Me. But when the *sun sets and* night falls, this work is impossible. ⁵Whenever I am in the world, I am the Light of the world.

⁶After He said these things, He spat on the ground and mixed saliva and dirt to form mud, which He smeared across the blind man's eyes.

Jesus (to the blind man): ⁷Go, wash yourself in the pool of Siloam.

Siloam means "sent," *and its name reminded us that his healing was sent by God.* The man went, washed, and returned to Jesus, his eyes now alive with sight. ⁸Then neighbors and others who knew him were confused to see a man so closely resembling the blind beggar running about.

Townspeople: Isn't this the man we see *every day* sitting and begging *in the streets?*

Others: ⁹This is the same man.

Still Others: This cannot be him. But this fellow bears an uncanny resemblance to the blind man.

Formerly Blind Man: I am the same man. *It's me!*

Townspeople: ¹⁰How have your *lifeless* eyes been opened?

Formerly Blind Man: ¹¹A man named Jesus *approached me and* made mud from the ground and applied it to my eyes. He then said to me, "Go, wash yourself in the pool of Siloam." I went and washed, and suddenly I could see.

Townspeople: ¹²Where is this man *who healed you?*

Formerly Blind Man: I don't know.

¹³⁻¹⁴The townspeople brought the formerly blind beggar to appear before the Pharisees *the same day Jesus healed him,* which happened to be on the Sabbath Day. ¹⁵The Pharisees began questioning him, looking for some explanation for how he could now see.

Formerly Blind Man: He smeared mud on my eyes, and I washed; now I see.

Some Pharisees: ¹⁶God can't possibly be behind this man because He is breaking the rules of the Sabbath.

Other Pharisees: How can such a lawbreaking scoundrel do something like this?

The Pharisees were at odds with one another about Jesus and could not agree *whether His power came from God or the devil.*

Pharisees (to the formerly blind man): ¹⁷What do you say about this man, about the fact He opened your eyes so you could see?

Formerly Blind Man: *I have no doubt*—this man is a prophet.

¹⁸Some of the Jews suspected the whole situation was a charade, that this man was never blind. So they summoned the man's parents to testify about his condition.

Pharisees: ¹⁹Is this man your son? Do you testify that he has been blind from birth? How therefore does he now see?

Parents: ²⁰We can tell you this much: he is our son, and he was born blind. ²¹But his new sight is a complete mystery to us! We do not know the man who opened his eyes. Why don't you ask our son? He is old enough to speak for himself.

²²The man's parents were a bit evasive because they were afraid of the Jewish leaders. It had been rumored that anyone who spoke of Jesus as the Anointed One would be expelled from the synagogue. ²³So they deferred the thorny question to their son, ²⁴and the Pharisees called on him a second time.

Pharisees: Give God the credit. *He's the One who healed you.* All glory belongs to God.

We are persuaded this man you speak of is a sinner *who defies God.*

Formerly Blind Man: 25If this man is a sinner, I don't know. *I am not qualified to say.* I only know one thing: I was blind, and now I see.

Pharisees: 26What did He do to you? How did He give you sight?

Formerly Blind Man: 27*Listen,* I've already answered all these questions, and you don't like my answers. Do you really need me to say it all over again? Are you thinking about joining up with Him and becoming His followers?

Pharisees (*berating him*): 28You're one of His followers, but we follow Moses. 29We have confidence that God spoke to Moses, but this man *you speak of is a mystery;* we don't even know where He comes from.

Formerly Blind Man: 30Isn't it ironic that you, *our religious leaders,* don't even know where He comes from; yet He gave me sight! 31We know that God does not listen to sinners, but He does respond and work through those who worship Him and do His will. 32No one has ever heard of someone opening the eyes of any person blind from birth. 33This man must come from God; otherwise, this miracle would not be possible. *Only God can do such things.*

Pharisees: 34You were born under a cloud of sin. How can you, *of all people,* lecture us?

The religious leaders banished him from their presence. 35Jesus heard what had happened and sought out the man.

Jesus: Do you believe in the Son of Man?

Formerly Blind Man: 36I want to believe, Lord. Who is He?

Jesus: 37You have seen His face *with your new eyes,* and you are talking to Him now.

Formerly Blind Man: 38Lord, I do believe.

The man bowed low to worship Jesus.

Jesus: 39I have entered this world to announce a verdict *that changes everything.*

Now those without sight may begin to see, and those who see may become blind.

Some Pharisees (*who overheard Jesus*): 40Surely we are not blind, are we?

Jesus: 41If you were blind, you would be without sin. But because you claim you can see, your sin is ever present.

The Pharisees are frequently around to challenge whatever Jesus says and does, but He always gets the better of them. Once again, Jesus turns what the Pharisees say inside out. They think blindness is a curse that evidences sin, and they think vision ensures knowledge and understanding—even concerning spiritual matters. Instead, the Pharisees' confidence in their vision and discernment make them unable to see the truth about Jesus. Ironically, they have blind trust in their sighted leaders. By refusing to believe in Him, they are the sinners—not the blind man.

---

10 **Jesus:** I tell you the truth: the man who crawls through the fence of the sheep pen, rather than walking through the gate, is a thief or a vandal. 2The shepherd walks openly through the entrance. 3The guard who is posted to protect the sheep opens the gate for the shepherd, and the sheep hear his voice. He calls his own sheep by name and leads them out. 4When all the sheep have been gathered, he walks on ahead of them; and they follow him because they know his voice. 5The sheep would not be willing to follow a stranger; they run because they do not know the voice of a stranger.

6Jesus explained a profound truth through this metaphor, but they did not understand His teaching. 7So He explained further.

Jesus: I tell you the truth: I am the gate of the sheep. 8All who approached the sheep before Me came as thieves and robbers, and the sheep did not listen to their voices. 9I am the gate; whoever enters through Me will be liberated, will go in and go out, and will find pastures. [10]The thief approaches *with malicious intent*, looking to steal, slaughter, and destroy; I came to give life with joy and abundance.

[11]I am the good shepherd. The good shepherd lays down His life for the sheep *in His care*. [12]The hired hand is not like the shepherd caring for His own sheep. When a wolf attacks, snatching and scattering the sheep, he runs for his life, leaving them *defenseless*. [13]The hired hand runs because he works only for wages and does not care for the sheep. [14]I am the good shepherd; I know My sheep, and My sheep know Me. [15]As the Father knows Me, I know the Father; I will give My life for the sheep. [16]There are many more sheep than you can see here, and I will bring them as well. They will hear My voice, and the flock will be united. One flock. One shepherd. [17]The Father loves Me because I *am willing to* lay down My life—but I will take it up again. [18]My life cannot be taken away by anybody else; I am giving it of My own free will. My authority allows Me to give My life and to take it again. All this has been commanded by My Father.

V

Jesus loves to explain truth through everyday things like vines, fruit, fishing, building, and shepherding, as He does here. He is a master communicator. In this metaphor, Jesus is the shepherd. Eventually He becomes the sheep as well. On the cross, He is destined to become the innocent sacrifice that makes all future sin sacrifices and burnt offerings unnecessary.

---

[19]When He spoke these words, some of the Jews began to argue.

Many Jews: [20]He has a demon and is a raving maniac. Why are you people listening to Him?

Other Jews: [21]No demon-possessed man ever spoke like this. Do demons give sight to the blind?

[22-23]It was winter and time for the Festival of Dedication.* While in Jerusalem, Jesus was walking through the temple in an area known as Solomon's porch, [24]and Jews gathered around Him.

Jews: How long are You going to keep us guessing? If You are God's Anointed, *the Liberating King,* announce it clearly.

Jesus: [25]I have told you, and you do not believe. The works I am doing in My Father's name tell the truth about Me. *You do not listen;* [26]you lack faith because you are not My sheep. [27]My sheep *respond as they* hear My voice; I know them *intimately,* and they follow Me. [28]I give them a life that is unceasing, and death will not have the last word. *Nothing or* no one can steal them from My hand. [29]My Father has given the flock to Me, and He is superior to all *beings and things.* No one is powerful enough to snatch the flock from My Father's hand. [30]The Father and I are one.

[31]The Jews gathered stones to execute Jesus right then and there.

Jesus: [32]I have performed many beautiful works before you in the name of the Father. Which of these can be judged as an offense that merits My execution?

Jews: [33]You are not condemned for performing miracles. We demand Your life because You are a man, yet you claim to be God. This is blasphemy!

Jesus: [34]*You know* what is written in the Scriptures. Doesn't it read, "I said, you are gods"?* [35]If the Scriptures called your ancestors (*mere mortals) gods to whom the word of God came—and the Scriptures cannot be set aside—[36]what should you call One *who is unique,* sanctified by and sent from the Father into the world? I have said, "I am God's Son." How can you call that blasphemy? [37]*By all means,* do not believe in Me, if I am not doing the things of the Father. [38]But examine My actions, *and you will see that My work is the work of the Father.* Regardless of whether you believe in Me—believe the miracles. Then you will know that the Father is in Me, and I am in the Father.

[39]Once again, *some of* the Jews tried to capture Him, but He slipped away, eluding their

* 10:22-23 The Festival of Lights or Hanukkah   * 10:34 Psalm 82:6

grasp. 40Jesus crossed the Jordan River and returned to the place where John was ritually cleansing the people through baptism* in the early days. He lingered in the area, 41and scores of people gathered around Him.

Crowds: John never performed any miracles, but every word he spoke about this man has come to pass. It is all true!

42In that place, many believed in Him.

V

John points to stories where Jesus returns to the issue of faith again and again. The crowds are fickle, believing sometimes and not others. The religious leaders refuse to believe because Jesus doesn't fit their paradigms. The disciples and close friends constantly face situations that challenge their faith, and this especially happens when Lazarus dies. John is implicitly urging his readers to have faith in Christ, even in difficult times, because He is the source of life and well being.

There was a certain man who was very ill. He was known as Lazarus from Bethany, which is the hometown of Mary and her sister Martha. 2Mary *did a beautiful thing for Jesus. She* anointed the Lord with a pleasant-smelling oil and wiped His feet with her hair. Her brother Lazarus became deathly ill, 3so the sisters immediately sent a message to Jesus which said, "Lord, the one You love is very ill." 4Jesus heard the message.

Jesus: His sickness will not end in his death but will bring great glory to God. As these events unfold, the Son of God will be exalted.

5Jesus *dearly* loved Mary, Martha, and Lazarus. 6However, after receiving this news, He waited two more days where He was.

Jesus (*speaking to the disciples*): 7It is time to return to Judea.

Disciples: 8Teacher, the last time You were there, some Jews attempted to execute You

by crushing You with stones. Why would You go back?

Jesus: 9There are 12 hours of daylight, correct? If anyone walks in the day, that person does not stumble because he or she sees the light of the world. 10If anyone walks at night, he will trip and fall because he does not have the light within. 11(Jesus briefly pauses.) Our friend Lazarus has gone to sleep, so I will go to awaken him.

Disciples: 12Lord, if he is sleeping, then he will be all right.

13Jesus used "sleep" *as a metaphor* for death, but the disciples took Him literally *and did not understand.* 14Then Jesus spoke plainly.

Jesus: Lazarus is dead, 15and I am grateful for your sakes that I was not there when he died. Now you will *see and* believe. Gather yourselves, and let's go to him.

Thomas, the Twin (*to the disciples*): 16Let's go so we can die with Him.

17-18As Jesus was approaching Bethany (which is about two miles east of Jerusalem), He heard that Lazarus had been in the tomb four days. 19Now many people had come to comfort Mary and Martha as they mourned the loss of their brother. 20Martha went to meet Jesus when word arrived that He was approaching Bethany, but Mary stayed behind at the house.

Martha: 21Lord, if You had been with us, my brother would not have died. 22Even so I still believe that anything You ask of God will be done.

Jesus: 23Your brother will rise to life.

Martha: 24I know. He will rise again when everyone is resurrected on the last day.

Jesus: 25I am the resurrection and the source of all life; those who believe in Me will live even in death. 26Everyone who lives and believes in Me will never truly die. Do you believe this?

Martha: 27Yes, Lord, I believe that You are the Anointed, *the Liberating King,* God's own Son who *we have heard* is coming into the world.

* 10:40 Literally, immersing, to show repentance

28After this Martha ran home to Mary.

Martha *(whispering to Mary)*: Come with me. The Teacher is here, and He has asked for you.

29Mary did not waste a minute. She got up and went 30to the same spot where Martha had found Jesus outside the village. 31The people gathered in her home offering support and comfort assumed she was going back to the tomb to cry and mourn, so they followed her. 32Mary approached Jesus, saw Him, and fell at His feet.

Mary: Lord, if only You had been here, my brother would still be alive.

33When Jesus saw Mary's *profound grief and the moaning and* weeping of her companions, He was deeply moved *by their pain* in His spirit and was intensely troubled.

Jesus: 34Where have you laid his body?

Jews: Come and see, Lord.

35*As they walked,* Jesus wept; 36and everyone noticed how much Jesus must have loved Lazarus. 37But others were skeptical.

Others: If this man can give sight to the blind, He could have kept him from dying.

They are asking, if Jesus loves Lazarus so much, why didn't He get here much sooner?

38Then Jesus, who was intensely troubled by all of this, approached the tomb—a *small* cave covered by a *massive* stone.

Jesus: 39Remove the stone.

Martha: Lord, he has been dead four days; the stench will be unbearable.

Jesus: 40Remember, I told you that if you believe, you will see the glory of God.

41They removed the stone, and Jesus lifted His eyes toward heaven.

Jesus: Father, I am grateful that You have heard Me. 42I know that You are always listening, but I proclaim it loudly so that everyone here will believe You have sent Me.

43After these words, He called out in a thunderous voice.

Jesus: Lazarus, come out!

44Then, the man who was dead walked out of his tomb bound from head to toe in a burial shroud.

Jesus: Untie him, and let him go.

Once again Jesus amazes everyone around Him. How does He raise Lazarus? What kind of man can speak life into death's darkness? Throughout His time on earth, those around Him are continually surprised by Jesus. He is unique. How does He have power over death? It takes a while, but more and more His followers become convinced this is no ordinary man.

45As a result, many of the Jews who had come with Mary saw what happened and believed in Him. 46But some went to the Pharisees to report what they witnessed Jesus doing. 47As a result of these reports—*and on short notice*—the chief priests and Pharisees called a meeting of the high council.

Pharisees: What are we going to do about this man? He is performing many miracles. 48If we don't stop this now, every man, woman, and child will believe in Him. *You know what will happen next? The Romans will think He's mounting a revolution and will destroy our temple. It will be the end of our nation.*

Caiaphas, the High Priest That Year: 49You have no idea what you are talking about; 50what you don't understand is that it's better for you that one man should die for the people so the whole nation won't perish.

51*His speech was more than it seemed.* As high priest that year, Caiaphas prophesied (without knowing it) that Jesus would die on behalf of the entire nation, 52and not just for the *children of* Israel—He would die so all God's children could be gathered from the four corners of the world into one people. [53]In that moment, they cemented their intentions to have Jesus executed.

[54]From that day forward, Jesus refrained from walking publicly among the people in Judea. He withdrew to a small town known as Ephraim, a rural area near the wilderness, where He set up camp with His disciples.

[55]The Passover was approaching, and Jews everywhere traveled to Jerusalem early so they could purify themselves and prepare for Passover. [56]People were looking for Jesus, hoping to catch a glimpse of Him in the city. All the while, some Jews were discussing Him in the temple.

Some Jews: Do you think He will decide not to come *to Jerusalem this year* for the feast?

[57]*In the midst of this confusion,* the Pharisees and the chief priests ordered that if anyone knew the whereabouts of Jesus *of Nazareth,* it must be reported immediately so they could arrest Him.

12 Six days before the Passover feast, Jesus journeyed to the village of Bethany, to the home of Lazarus who had recently been raised from the dead, [2]where they hosted Him for dinner. Martha was busy serving *as the hostess,* Lazarus reclined at the table with Him, [3]and Mary took a pound of fine ointment, pure nard (which is *both rare and* expensive), and anointed Jesus' feet with it; and then she wiped them with her hair. As the pleasant fragrance of this extravagant ointment filled the entire house, [4]Judas Iscariot, one of His disciples (who was plotting to betray Jesus), began to speak.

Judas Iscariot: [5]*How could she pour out* this vast amount of fine oil? Why didn't she sell it? It is worth nearly a year's wages;* the money could have been given to the poor.

[6]This had nothing to do with Judas's desire to help the poor. The truth is he served as the treasurer, and he helped himself to the money from the common pot at every opportunity.

Jesus: [7]Leave her alone. She has observed this custom in anticipation of the day of My burial. [8]The poor are ever present, but I will be leaving.

[9]Word spread of Jesus' presence, and a large crowd was gathering to see Jesus and the formerly deceased Lazarus, whom He had brought back from the dead. [10]The chief priests were secretly plotting Lazarus's murder since, [11]because of him, many Jews were leaving their teachings and believing in Jesus.

[12]The next day, a great crowd of people who had come to the festival heard that Jesus was coming to Jerusalem; [13]so they gathered branches of palm trees to wave as they celebrated His arrival.

Crowds (*shouting*): Hosanna!
He who comes in the name of the Lord is truly blessed*
and is King of all Israel.

[14]Jesus found a young donkey, sat on it, *and rode through the crowds mounted on this small beast.* The Scriptures foretold of this day:

[15]Daughter of Zion, do not be afraid.
Watch! Your King is coming.
You will find Him seated on the colt of a donkey.*

[16]The disciples did not understand any of this at the time; these truths did not sink in until Jesus had been glorified. As they reflected on their memories of Jesus, they realized these things happened just as they were written. [17]Those who witnessed the resurrection of Lazarus enthusiastically spoke of Jesus to all who would listen, [18]and that is why the crowd went out to meet Him. They had heard of the miraculous sign He had done.

His followers may suspect during their time with Jesus that He is more than a man, but it takes the power and glory of the resurrection to convince them completely that Jesus is divine. When they see Him, touch Him, and hear the sound of His voice thunder in their souls, the disciples know they are face-to-face with God's immense glory, the unique Son of God. Reading

* 12:5 Literally, 300 denarii, Roman coins   * 12:13 Psalm 118:26
* 12:15 Zechariah 9:9

and rereading the Scriptures in light of their experiences of Him, it becomes clear that Jesus' life and story are the climax of God's covenants with His people.

Pharisees (to one another): ¹⁹Our efforts to squelch Him have not worked, *but now is not the time for action.* Look, the world is following after Him.

²⁰Among the crowds traveling to Jerusalem were Greeks seeking to *follow God and* worship at the great feast. ²¹⁻²²Some of them came to Philip with an important request.

Greek Pilgrims (to Philip): Sir, we are hoping to meet Jesus.

Philip, a disciple from the Galilean village of Bethsaida, told Andrew *that these Greeks wanted to see Jesus.* Together Andrew and Philip approached Jesus to inform Him about the request.

Jesus (to Philip and Andrew): ²³The time has come for the Son of Man to be glorified. ²⁴I tell you the truth: unless a grain of wheat is planted in the ground and dies, it remains a solitary seed. But when it is planted, it produces in death a great harvest. ²⁵The one who loves this life will lose it, and the one who despises it in this world will have life forevermore. ²⁶Anyone who serves Me must follow My path; anyone who serves Me will want to be where I am, and he will be honored by the Father. ²⁷My spirit is low and unsettled. How can I ask the Father to save Me from this hour? This hour is the purpose for which I have come *into the world. But what I can say is this:* ²⁸"Father, glorify Your name!"

Suddenly a voice echoed from the heavens.

The Father: I have glorified My name. And again I will bring glory *in this hour that will resound throughout time.*

²⁹The crowd of people surrounding Jesus were confused.

Some in the Crowd: It sounded like thunder.

Others: A heavenly messenger spoke to Him.

Jesus: ³⁰The voice you hear has not spoken for My benefit, but for yours. ³¹Now judgment comes upon this world, *and everything will change.* The tyrant of this world, *Satan,* will be thrown out. ³²When I am lifted up from the earth, then all of humanity will be drawn to Me.

³³These words foreshadowed the nature of His death.

Crowd: ³⁴The law teaches that the Anointed is the One who will remain without end. How can You say it is essential that the Son of Man be lifted up? Who is this Son of Man *You are talking about?*

Jesus: ³⁵Light is among you, but very soon it will flicker out. Walk as you have the light, and then the darkness will not surround you. Those who walk in darkness don't know where they are going. ³⁶While the light is with you, believe in the light; and you will be reborn as sons *and daughters* of the light.

After speaking these words, Jesus left the people to go to a place of seclusion. ³⁷Despite all the signs He performed, they still did not believe in Him. ³⁸Isaiah spoke of this reality, saying,

> Lord, who could accept what we've been told?
> And who has seen the awesome power of the Lord revealed?*

³⁹This is the reason they are unable to believe. ⁴⁰Isaiah also said,

> God has blinded their eyes
> and hardened their hearts
> So that their eyes cannot see *properly*
> and their hearts cannot understand
> *and be persuaded*
> *by the truth* to turn to Me
> and be reconciled by My healing hand.*

⁴¹Isaiah could say this because he had seen the glory of the Lord *with his own eyes* and declared His beauty aloud. ⁴²Yet many leaders secretly believed in Him but would not declare their faith because the Pharisees continued their threats to expel all His

* 12:38 Isaiah 53:1   * 12:40 Isaiah 6:10

followers from the synagogue; [43]here's why: they loved to please men more than they desired to glorify God.

Jesus (crying out before the people): [44]Anyone who believes in Me is not placing his faith in Me, but in the One who sent Me here. [45]If one sees Me, he sees the One who sent Me. [46]I am here to bring light in this world, freeing everyone who believes in Me from the darkness that blinds him. [47]If anyone listening to My teachings chooses to ignore them, so be it: I have come to liberate the world, not to judge it. [48]However, those who reject Me and My teachings will be judged: in the last day, My words will be their judge [49]because I am not speaking of My own volition and from My own authority. The Father who sent Me has commanded Me what to say and speak. [50]I know His command is eternal life, so every word I utter originates in Him.

13 Before the Passover festival began, Jesus was keenly aware that His hour had come to depart from this world and to return to the Father. From beginning to end, Jesus' days were marked by His love for His people. [2]Before Jesus and His disciples gathered for dinner, the adversary filled Judas Iscariot's heart with plans of deceit and betrayal. [3]Jesus, knowing that He had come from God and was going away to God, [4]stood up from dinner and removed His outer garments. He then wrapped Himself in a towel, [5]poured water in a basin, and began to wash the feet of the disciples, drying them with His towel.

Simon Peter (as Jesus approaches): [6]Lord, are You going to wash my feet?

Jesus: [7]Peter, you don't realize what I am doing, but you will understand later.

Peter: [8]You will not wash my feet, now or ever!

Jesus: If I don't wash you, you will have nothing to do with Me.

Peter: [9]Then wash me but don't stop with my feet. Cleanse my hands and head as well.

Jesus: [10]Listen, anyone who has bathed is clean all over except for the feet. But I tell you this, not all of you are clean.

Within pain and filth, there is an opportunity to extend God's kingdom through an expression of love, humility, and service. This simple act of washing feet is a metaphor for how the world looks through the lens of Jesus' grace. He sees the people—the world He created—which He loves. He also sees the filthy corruption in the world that torments everyone. His mission is to cleanse those whom He loves from those horrors. This is His redemptive work with feet, families, disease, famine, and hearts.

When Jesus sees disease, He sees the opportunity to heal. When He sees sin, He sees a chance to forgive and redeem. When He sees dirty feet, He sees a chance to wash them.

[11]He knew the one with plans of betraying Him, which is why He said, "not all of you are clean." [12]After washing their feet and picking up His garments, He reclined at the table again.

Jesus: Do you understand what I have done to you? [13]You call Me Teacher and Lord, and truly, that is who I am. [14]So if your Lord and Teacher washes your feet, then you should wash one another's feet. [15]I am your example; keep doing what I do. [16]I tell you the truth: a servant is not greater than the master. Those who are sent are not greater than the one who sends them.* [17]If you know these things, and if you put them into practice, you will find happiness. [18]I am not speaking about all of you. I know whom I have chosen, but let the Hebrew Scripture be fulfilled that says, "The very same man who eats My bread with Me will stab Me in the back." [19]Assuredly, I tell you these truths before they happen so that when it all transpires, you will believe that I am. [20]I tell you the truth: anyone who accepts the ones I send accepts Me. In turn, the ones who accept Me also accept the One who sent Me.

[21]Jesus was becoming visibly distressed.

* 13:16 Literally, apostle

Jesus: I tell you the truth: one of you will betray Me.

22The disciples began to stare at one another, wondering who was the unfaithful disciple. 23One disciple in particular, who was loved by Jesus, reclined next to Him at the table. 24Peter motioned to the disciple at Jesus' side.

Peter (to the beloved disciple): Find out who the betrayer is.

Beloved Disciple (leaning in to Jesus): 25Lord, who is it?

Jesus: 26I will dip a piece of bread in My cup and give it to the one who will betray Me.

He dipped one piece in the cup and gave it to Judas, the son of Simon Iscariot. 27After this occurred, Satan entered into Judas.

Jesus (to Judas): Make haste, and do what you are going to do.

28No one understood Jesus' instructions to Judas. 29Because Judas carried the money, some thought he was being instructed to buy the necessary items for the feast or give some money to the poor. 30So Judas took his piece of bread and departed into the night. 31Upon Judas's departure, Jesus spoke:

Jesus: Now the Son of Man will be glorified as God is glorified in Him. 32If God's glory is in Him, His glory is also in God. The moment of this astounding glory is imminent. 33My children, My time here is brief. You will be searching for Me; and as I told the Jews, "You cannot go where I am going." 34So I give you a new command: Love each other *deeply and fully*. Remember the ways that I have loved you, and demonstrate your love for others in those same ways. 35Everyone will know you as My followers if you demonstrate your love to others.

Simon Peter: 36Lord, where are You going?

Jesus: Peter, you cannot come with Me now, but later you will join Me.

Peter: 37Why can't I go now? I'll give my life for You!

Jesus: 38Will you really give your life for Me? I tell you the truth: you will deny Me three times before the rooster crows.

Ultimately Peter is telling the truth. He is more than willing to lay down his life. But none of His disciples understand the magnitude of the persecution and hatred that is about to be unleashed.

Even Peter, Jesus' dear Peter, is afraid. He protests any inference to Jesus' impending departure. Each of the twelve would do the same. Jesus calms their fears over and over again with stories, metaphors, and outright promises, saying, "I will never abandon you like orphans; I will return to be with you" (14:18).

---

14 **Jesus:** Don't get lost in despair; believe in God, and keep on believing in Me. 2My Father's home is designed to accommodate all of you. If there were not room for everyone, I would have told you that. I am going to make arrangements for your arrival. 3I will be there to greet you personally and welcome you home, where we will be together. 4You know where I am going and how to get there.

Thomas: 5Lord, we don't know where You are going, so how can we know the path?

Jesus: 6I am the path, the truth, and the *energy of* life. No one comes to the Father except through Me. 7If you know Me, you know the Father. Rest assured now; you know Him and have seen Him.

Philip: 8Lord, all I am asking is that You show us the Father.

Jesus (to Philip): 9I have lived with you all this time, and you still don't know who I am? If you have seen Me, you have seen the Father. How can you keep asking to see the Father? 10Don't you believe Me when I say I abide in the Father and the Father dwells in Me? I'm not making this up as I go along. The Father has given Me these truths that I have been speaking to you, and

He empowers all My actions. [11]Accept these truths: I am in the Father, and the Father is in Me. If you have trouble believing based on My words, believe because of the things I have done. [12]I tell you the truth: whoever believes in Me will be able to do what I have done, but they will do even greater things, because I will return to be with the Father. [13]Whatever you ask for in My name, I will do it so that the Father will get glory from the Son. [14]*Let Me say it again:* if you ask for anything in My name, I will do it. [15]If you love Me, obey the commandments I have given you. [16]I will ask the Father to send you another Helper, *the Spirit of truth,* who will remain constantly with you. [17]The world does not recognize the Spirit of truth, because it does not know the Spirit and is unable to receive Him. But you do know the Spirit because He lives with you, and He will dwell in you. [18]I will never abandon you like orphans; I will return to be with you. [19]In a little while, the world will not see Me; but I will not vanish completely from your sight. Because I live, you will also live. [20]At that time, you will know that I am in the Father, you are in Me, and I am in you. [21]The one who loves Me will do the things I have commanded. My Father loves everyone who loves Me; and I will love you and reveal My heart, will, and nature to you.

The Other Judas: [22]Lord, why will You reveal Yourself to us, but not to the world?

Jesus: [23]Anyone who loves Me will listen to My voice and obey. The Father will love him, and We will draw close to him and make a dwelling place within him. [24]The one who does not love Me ignores My message, which is not from Me, but from the Father who sent Me.

[25]I have spoken these words while I am here with you. [26]The Father is sending a great Helper, the Holy Spirit, in My name to teach you everything and to remind you of all I have said to you. [27]My peace is the legacy I leave to you. I don't give gifts like those of this world. Do not let your heart be troubled or fearful. [28]You were listening when I said, "I will go away, but I will also return to be with you." If you love Me, celebrate the fact that I am going to be with the Father because He is far greater than I am. [29]I have told you all these things in advance so that your faith will grow as these things come to pass. [30]I am almost finished speaking to you. The one who rules the world is stepping forward, and he has no part in Me; [31]but to demonstrate to the cosmos My love for the Father, I will do just as He commands. Stand up. It is time for us to leave this place.

V

15 **Jesus:** I am the true vine, and My Father is the keeper of the vineyard. [2]My Father examines every branch in Me and cuts away those who do not bear fruit. He leaves those bearing fruit and carefully prunes them so that they will bear more fruit; [3]already you are clean because you have heard My voice. [4]Abide in Me, and I will abide in you. A branch cannot bear fruit if it is disconnected from the vine, and neither will you if you are not connected to Me.

[5]I am the vine, and you are the branches. If you abide in Me and I in you, you will bear great fruit. Without Me, you will accomplish nothing. [6]If anyone does not abide in Me, he is like a branch that is tossed out and shrivels up and is later gathered to be tossed into the fire to burn. [7]If you abide in Me and My voice abides in you, anything you ask will come to pass for you. [8]Your abundant growth and your faithfulness as My followers will bring glory to the Father.

God becomes flesh and lives among humanity, not just to have a transaction with people and ultimately die, but to continue to be with them and to send His Spirit to be present with believers. So God calls His Spirit-indwelled people to something greater, something more significant: they are here as redeeming forces on this earth; their time here is about reclaiming the things He has created. Believing God has created the entire cosmos and that it is restored in Jesus, the believer's work here through the Spirit is to say, "This belongs to God," and to help point out the beauty of creation to everyone. And most of all, to live in it themselves by the power of the Holy Spirit who plants the teachings of the Lord in their hearts.

> **V**
> At a time when all of His disciples are feeling as if they are about to be uprooted, Jesus sketches a picture of this new life as a flourishing vineyard—a labyrinth of vines and strong branches steeped in rich soil, abundant grapes hanging from their vines ripening in the sun. Jesus sculpts a new garden of Eden in their imaginations—one that is bustling with fruit, sustenance, and satisfying aromas. This is the Kingdom life. It is all about connection, sustenance, and beauty. But within this promise of life is the warning that people must be in Christ or they will not experience these blessings.

Jesus: [9]I have loved you as the Father has loved Me. Abide in My love. [10]Follow My example in obeying the Father's commandments and receiving His love. If you obey My commandments, you will stay in My love. [11]I want you to know the delight I experience, to find ultimate satisfaction, which is why I am telling you all of this.

[12]My commandment to you is this: love others as I have loved you. [13]There is no greater way to love than to give your life for your friends. [14]You celebrate our friendship if you obey this command. [15]I don't call you servants any longer; servants don't know what the master is doing, but I have told you everything the Father has said to Me. I call you friends. [16]You did not choose Me. I chose you, and I orchestrated all of this so that you would be sent out and bear great and perpetual fruit. As you do this, anything you ask the Father in My name will be done. [17]This is My command to you: love one another.

[18]If you find that the world despises you, remember that before it despised you, it first despised Me. [19]If you were a product of the world order, then it would love you. But you are not a product of the world because I have taken you out of it, and it despises you for that very reason. [20]Don't forget what I have spoken to you: "a servant is not greater than the master." If I was mistreated, you should expect nothing less. If they accepted what I have spoken, they will also hear you. [21]Everything

they do to you they will do on My account because they do not know the One who has sent Me. [22]If I had not spoken within their hearing, they would not be guilty of sin; but now they have no excuse for ignoring My voice.

[23]If someone despises Me, he also despises My Father. [24]If I had not demonstrated things for them that have never been done, they would not be guilty of sin. But the reality is they have stared Me in the face, and they have despised Me and the Father nonetheless. [25]Yet their law, which says, "They despised Me without any cause,"* has again been proven true.

[26]I will send a great Helper to you from the Father, one known as the Spirit of truth. He comes from the Father and will point to the truth as it concerns Me. [27]But you will also point others to the truth about My identity, because you have journeyed with Me since this all began.

> **V**
> As Jesus warns of the mistreatment His followers can expect, He disarms fears by noting the most important things. If the Spirit is within, there is no reason to fear. In fact, the church will thrive under persecution. Yet humans are obsessed with power and political prominence as a means to influence the culture. Christian citizens have an obligation to strive for justice and freedom through the transforming power of the Spirit in people's lives. Rather than exerting temporal power, the real work of the Kingdom often thrives under fierce attack and opposition. Jesus announces this coming persecution to His followers, believing this will lead to their finest hour.

16 **Jesus:** I am telling you all of this so that you may avoid the offenses that are coming. [2]The time will come when they will kick you out of the synagogue because some believe God desires them to execute you as an act of faithful service. [3]They will do this because they don't know the Father, or else they

* 15:25 Psalm 35:19

would know Me. [4]I'm telling you all this so that when it comes to pass you will remember what you have heard. It was not important for Me to give you this information in the beginning when I was with you. [5]But now, I am going to the One who has sent Me, and none of you ask Me, "Where are You going?"

[6]I know that hearing news like this is overwhelming and sad. [7]But the truth is that My departure will be a gift that will serve you well, because if I don't leave, the great Helper will not come to your aid. When I leave, I will send Him to you. [8-9]When He arrives, He will uncover the sins of the world, expose unbelief as sin, and allow all to see their sins in the light of righteousness for the first time. [10]This new awareness of righteousness is important because I am going to the Father and will no longer be present with you. [11]The Spirit will also carry My judgment because the one who rules in this world has already been defeated.

[12]I have so much more to say, but you cannot absorb it right now. [13-15]The Spirit of truth will come and guide you in all truth. He will not speak His own words to you; He will speak what He hears, revealing to you the things to come and bringing glory to Me. The Spirit has unlimited access to Me, to all that I possess and know, just as everything the Father has is Mine. That is the reason I am confident He will care for My own and reveal the path to you. [16]For a little while you will not see Me; but after that, a time will come when you will see Me again.

Some of His Disciples: [17]What does He mean? "I'll be here, and then I won't be here, because I'll be with the Father"?

Other Disciples: [18]What is He saying? "A little while"? We don't understand.

The promise of eternity is a reminder that God's children are made for a renewed world. There is great comfort amid fear, knowing believers will be reunited with Jesus and joined with the Father. As believers labor together in this world—enduring pain, loss, and unfulfilled desires—they should be encouraged that in eternity all needs will be fulfilled in the presence of God.

[19]Jesus knew they had questions to ask of Him, so He approached them.

Jesus: Are you trying to figure out what I mean when I say you will see Me in a little while? [20]I tell you the truth, a time is approaching when you will weep and mourn while the world is celebrating. You will grieve, but that grief will give birth to great joy. [21-22]In the same way that a woman labors in great pain during childbirth only to forget the intensity of the pain when she holds her child, when I return, your labored grief will also change into a joy that cannot be stolen.

[23]When all this transpires, you will finally have the answers you have been seeking. I tell you the truth, anything you ask of the Father in My name, He will give to you. [24]Until this moment, you have not sought after anything in My name. Ask and you will receive so that you will be filled with joy.

[25]I have been teaching you all of these truths through stories and metaphors, but the time is coming for Me to speak openly and directly of the Father.

[26]The day is coming when you will make a request in My name, but I will not represent you before the Father. [27]*You will be heard directly by the Father.* The Father loves you because you love Me and know that I come from the Father. [28]I came from the Father into the cosmos, but soon I will leave it and return to the Father.

All His disciples mourn Jesus' refusal to take His rightful place as a king and lead a revolution. Jesus knows political might, brute force, and earthly governments are not helpful tools in a battle for hearts. Spiritual revolutions are subversive. They are led by defiant acts of love (for example, healing, foot washing, and martyrdom). Laws do not change hearts, and violence induces hatred and fear. But a sincere community of faith in which love and hope are demonstrated even in the darkest hours will lead a spiritual revolution. It is time to go forward with open eyes and continue to labor as Christian citizens, placing hope only in the redemptive work of the gospel.

Disciples: [29]We hear You speaking clearly and not in metaphors. *How could we misunderstand?* [30]We see now that You are aware of everything and You reveal things at the proper time. So we do not need to question You, because we believe You have come from God.

Jesus: [31]So you believe now? [32]Be aware that a time is coming when you will be scattered *like seeds*. You will return to your own way, and I will be left alone. But I will not be alone, because the Father will be with Me. [33]I have told you these things so that you will be *whole and* at peace. In this world, you will be plagued with times of trouble, but you need not fear; I have triumphed over this corrupt world order.

17 **Jesus** (*lifting His face to the heavens*): Father, My time has come. Glorify Your Son, and I will bring You great glory [2-3]because You have given Me total authority over humanity. *I have come bearing the plentiful gifts of God;* and all who receive Me will experience everlasting life, a new intimate relationship with You (the one True God) and Jesus the Anointed (the One You have sent). [4]I have glorified You on earth and fulfilled the mission You set before Me.

[5]In this moment, Father, fuse Our collective glory and bring Us together as We were before creation existed. [6]You have entrusted Me with these men who have come out of this corrupt world order. I have told them about Your nature and declared Your name to them, and they have held on to Your words and understood that these words, [7]like everything else You have given Me, come from You. [8]It is true that these men You gave Me have received the words that come from You and not only understood them but also believed that You sent Me. [9]I am now making an appeal to You on their behalf. This request is not for the entire world; it is for those whom You have given to Me because they are Yours.

[10]Yours and Mine, Mine and Yours, for all that are Mine are Yours. Through them I have been glorified.

[11]I will no longer be physically present in this world, but they will remain in this world. As I return to be with You, holy Father, remain with them through Your name, *the name You have given Me.* May they be one even as We are one. [12]While I was physically present with them, I protected them through Your name. I watched over them closely; and only one was lost, the one the Scriptures said was the son of destruction. [13]Now I am returning to You. I am speaking this prayer here in the created cosmos *alongside friends and foes* so that in hearing it they might be consumed with joy. [14]I have given them Your word; and the world has despised them because they are not products of the world, in the same way that I am not a product of the corrupt world order. [15]Do not take them out of this world; protect them from the evil one.

[16]Like Me, they are not products of the corrupt world order. [17]Immerse them in the truth, the truth Your voice speaks. [18]In the same way You sent Me into this world, I am sending them. [19]It is entirely for their benefit that I have set Myself apart so that they may be set apart by truth. [20]I am not asking solely for their benefit; this prayer is also for all the believers who will follow them and hear them speak. [21]Father, may they all be one as You are in Me and I am in You; may they be in Us, for by this unity world will believe that You sent Me.

[22]All the glory You have given to Me, I pass on to them. May that glory unify them and make them one as We are one, [23]I in them and You in Me, that they may be refined so that all will know that You sent Me, and You love them in the same way You love Me.

In this great prayer that Jesus prays for His disciples, He returns repeatedly to the gathering of believers unified with the Father and the Son.

[24]Father, I long for the time when those You have given Me can join Me in My place so they may witness My glory, which comes from You. You have loved Me before the foundations of the cosmos were laid. [25]Father, You are just; though this corrupt world order does not know You, I do.

These followers know that You have sent Me. ²⁶I have told them about Your nature; and I will continue to speak of Your name in order that Your love, which was poured out on Me, will be in them. And I will also be in them.

18 When Jesus finished praying, He began a brief journey with His disciples to the other side of the Kidron Valley, a deep ravine that floods in the winter rains, then farther on to a garden where He gathered His disciples.

²⁻³Judas Iscariot (who had already set his betrayal in motion and knew that Jesus often met with the disciples in this olive grove) entered the garden with an entourage of Roman soldiers and officials sent by the chief priests and Pharisees. They brandished their weapons under the light of torches and lamps. ⁴Jesus stepped forward. It was clear He was not surprised because He knew all things.

Jesus: Whom are you looking for?

Judas's Entourage: ⁵Jesus the Nazarene.

Jesus: I am the One.

Judas, the betrayer, stood with the military force. ⁶As Jesus spoke "I am the One," the forces fell back on the ground. ⁷Jesus asked them a second time:

Jesus: Whom are you searching for?

Judas's Entourage: Jesus the Nazarene.

Jesus: ⁸I have already said that I am the One. If you are looking for Me, then let these men go free.

⁹This happened to fulfill the promise He made that none of those entrusted to Him will be lost.* ¹⁰Suddenly Peter lunged toward Malchus, one of the high priest's servants; and with his sword, Peter severed the man's right ear.

Jesus (to Peter): ¹¹Put down your sword, and return it to the sheath. Am I to turn away from the cup the Father has given Me to drink?

¹²So the Roman commander, soldiers, and Jewish officials arrested Jesus, cuffed His hands and feet, ¹³and brought Him to Annas

(the father-in-law of Caiaphas the high priest). ¹⁴You may remember that Caiaphas counseled the Jews that one should die for all people. ¹⁵⁻¹⁶Simon Peter and another disciple followed behind Jesus. When they arrived, Peter waited in the doorway while the other disciple was granted access because of his relationship with the high priest. That disciple spoke to the woman at the door, and Peter was allowed inside.

Servant Girl (to Peter): ¹⁷You are one of this man's disciples, aren't you?

Peter: I am not.

¹⁸All the servants and officers gathered around a charcoal fire to keep warm. It was a cold day, and Peter made his way into the circle to warm himself.

Annas (to Jesus): ¹⁹Who are Your disciples, and what do You teach?

Jesus: ²⁰I have spoken in public where the world can hear, always teaching in the synagogue and in the temple where the Jewish people gather. I have never spoken in secret. ²¹So why would you need to interrogate Me? Many have heard Me teach. Why don't you question them? They know what I have taught.

²²While Jesus offered His response, an officer standing nearby struck Jesus with his hand.

Officer: Is that how You speak to the high priest?

Jesus: ²³If I have spoken incorrectly, why don't you point out the untruths that I speak? Why do you hit Me if what I have said is correct?

²⁴Annas sent Jesus to Caiaphas bound as a prisoner. ²⁵As this was happening, Peter was still warming himself by the fire.

Servants and Officers: You, too, are one of His disciples, aren't you?

Peter: No, I am not.

²⁶One of the high priest's servants who was related to *Malchus*—the person Peter *attacked and* cut off his ear—*recognized Peter.*

* 18:9 John 6:39

Initially, Pilate tells the Jewish leaders to take Jesus and try Him according to Jewish law, but when they hint at capital charges, Pilate agrees to interrogate Jesus as a traitor to the empire. Rome reserves the right to decide who lives and dies in the provinces. They don't delegate that to the Jewish high council. The charge of blasphemy carries no weight in Roman jurisprudence, for it is a matter of Jewish religious law. Rome has no opinion on such matters. So a new charge must be concocted, a charge that Rome does care about. Rome does care about taxes, of course, and takes a dim view of anyone making royal claims under their noses.

Pilate agrees to hear the charge, not wasting a Roman minute. He takes Jesus inside and begins asking Him about these charges. Pilate can't handle the truth when he asks, "Are You the King of the Jews?" Jesus is the King of the Jews, and that is the truth. But as Jesus knows, the world doesn't recognize His kingdom. That's because it is sourced in heaven above, not in Rome. His authority comes from God the Father, Creator, Sustainer—not from the Roman senate.

High Priest's Servant: Didn't I see you in the garden with Him?

27Peter denied it again, and instantly a rooster crowed.

28Before the sun had risen, Jesus was taken from Caiaphas to the governor's palace. The Jewish leaders would not enter the palace because their presence in a Roman office would defile them and cause them to miss the Passover feast. Pilate, the governor, met them outside.

Now Caiaphas is high priest at this time. The sacred office he occupies has been corrupted for more than a century by Jewish collaboration with Greeks and Romans. Reformers are few, and they have been unable to cleanse the high office from its pollutants. Because of this, many Jews have stopped coming to the temple. How can God's holy habitation on earth be pure if its primary representative is coddling the enemies of Israel? Caiaphas knows he needs friends in high places to put an end to Jesus, so he turns to Pilate, the Roman governor. It is Pilate's job to look out for Roman interests in Judea. He is an irritable man, unnecessarily cruel and intentionally provocative. Many Jews will die on his watch. For Pilate, Jesus is just one more.

Pilate: 29What charges do you bring against this man?

Priests and Officials: 30If He weren't a lawbreaker, we wouldn't have brought Him to you.

Pilate: 31Then judge Him yourselves, by your own law.

Jews: Our authority does not allow us to give Him the death penalty.

32All these things were a fulfillment of the words Jesus had spoken indicating the way that He would die. 33So Pilate reentered the governor's palace and called for Jesus to follow him.

Pilate: Are You the King of the Jews?

Jesus: 34Are you asking Me because you believe this is true, or have others said this about Me?

Pilate: 35I'm not a Jew, am I? Your people, including the chief priests, have arrested You and placed You in my custody. What have You done?

Jesus: 36My kingdom is not recognized in this world. If this were My kingdom, My servants would be fighting for My freedom. But My kingdom is not in this physical realm.

Pilate: 37So You are a king?

Jesus: You say that I am king. For this I have been born, and for this I have come into the cosmos: to demonstrate the power of truth. Everyone who seeks truth hears My voice.

Pilate *(to Jesus)*: ³⁸What is truth?

Pilate left Jesus to go and speak to the Jewish people.

Pilate *(to the Jews)*: I have not found any cause for charges to be brought against this man. ³⁹Your custom is that I should release a prisoner to you each year in honor of the Passover celebration; shall I release the King of the Jews to you?

Jews: ⁴⁰No, not this man! Give us Barabbas!

You should know that Barabbas was a terrorist.

19 Pilate took Jesus and had Him flogged. ²The soldiers twisted thorny branches together as a crown and placed it onto His brow and wrapped Him in a purple cloth. ³They drew near to Him, shouting:

Soldiers *(striking at Jesus)*: Bow down, everyone! This is the King of the Jews!

Pilate *(going out to the crowd)*: ⁴Listen, I stand in front of you with this man to make myself clear: I find this man innocent of any crimes.

⁵Then Jesus was paraded out before the people, wearing the crown of thorns and the purple robe.

Pilate: Here is the man!

Chief Priests and Officers *(shouting)*: ⁶Crucify, crucify!

Pilate: You take Him and crucify Him; I have declared Him not guilty of any punishable crime!

Jews: ⁷Our law says that He should die because He claims to be the Son of God.

⁸Pilate was terrified to hear the Jews making their claims for His execution; ⁹so he retired to his court, the Praetorium.

Pilate *(to Jesus)*: Where are You from?

Jesus did not speak.

Pilate: ¹⁰How can You ignore me? Are You not aware that I have the authority either to free You or to crucify You?

Jesus: ¹¹Any authority you have over Me comes from above, not from your political position. Because of this, the one who handed Me to you is guilty of the greater sin.

¹²Pilate listened to Jesus' words. Taking them to heart, he attempted to release Jesus; but the Jews opposed him, shouting:

Jews: If you release this man, you have betrayed Caesar. Anyone who claims to be a king threatens Caesar's throne.

¹³After Pilate heard these accusations, he sent Jesus out and took his seat in the place where he rendered judgment. This place was called the Pavement, or Gabbatha in Hebrew. ¹⁴All this occurred at the sixth hour on the day everyone prepares for the Passover.

Pilate *(to the Jews)*: Look, here is your King!

Jews: ¹⁵Put Him away; crucify Him!

Pilate: You want me to crucify your King?

Chief Priests: We have no king but Caesar!

¹⁶Pilate handed Him over to his soldiers, knowing that He would be crucified. ¹⁷They sent Jesus out carrying His own instrument of execution, the cross, to a hill known as the Place of the Skull, or Golgotha in Hebrew. ¹⁸In that place, they crucified Him along with two others. One was on His right and the other on His left. ¹⁹Pilate ordered that a plaque be placed above Jesus' head. It read, "Jesus of Nazareth, the King of the Jews." ²⁰Because the site was near an urban region, it was written in three languages (Greek, Latin, and Hebrew) so that all could understand.

Chief Priests *(to Pilate)*: ²¹Don't write, "The King of the Jews." Write, "He said, 'I am King of the Jews'!"

Pilate: ²²I have written what I have written.

²³As Jesus was being crucified, the soldiers tore His outer garments into four pieces,

one for each of them. They wanted to do the same with His tunic, but it was seamless—one piece of fabric woven from the top down. [24]So they said,

Soldier (*to other soldiers*): Don't tear it. Let's cast lots, and the winner will take the whole thing.

This happened in keeping with the Hebrew Scriptures, which said, "They divided My outer garments and cast lots for My clothes."* These soldiers did exactly what was foretold in the Hebrew Scriptures. [25]Jesus' mother was standing next to His cross along with her sister, Mary the wife of Clopas, and Mary Magdalene. [26]Jesus looked to see His mother and the disciple He loved standing nearby.

Jesus (*to Mary, His mother*): Dear woman, this is your son (*motioning to the beloved disciple*)! [27](to *John*, His disciple) This is now your mother.

V

Now you know who "the beloved disciple" is: the last eyewitness to the life, death, and resurrection of Jesus. Mary has become family to John, fulfilling the dying wish of Jesus, his Savior. For those who are gathered at the foot of the cross, family is less about blood kinship than it is about covenant obedience.

The mother of the Lord will serve the redemptive purposes of her son and the Savior of the world until her last day on earth. Anyone feeling sorry for himself should think about Jesus. He spent all this time before His death, and through His death, demonstrating how to love and how to serve. He is asking John to do no more in serving Mary than He did in serving us.

From that moment, the disciple treated her like his own mother and welcomed her into his house. [28]Jesus knew now that His work had been accomplished, and the Hebrew Scriptures were being fulfilled.

Jesus: I am thirsty.

[29]A jar of sour wine had been left there, so they took a hyssop branch with a sponge soaked in the vinegar and put it to His mouth. [30]When Jesus drank, He spoke:

Jesus: It is finished!

In that moment, His head fell; and He gave up the spirit. [31]The Jews asked Pilate to have their legs broken so the bodies would not remain on the crosses on the Sabbath. It was the day of preparation for the Passover, and that year the Passover fell on the Sabbath. [32]The soldiers came and broke the legs of both the men crucified next to Jesus. [33]When they came up to Jesus' cross, they could see that He was dead; so they did not break His legs. [34]Instead, one soldier took his spear and pierced His abdomen, which brought a gush of blood and water.

[35]This testimony is true. In fact, it is an eyewitness account; and he has reported what he saw so that you also may believe. [36]It happened this way to fulfill the Hebrew Scriptures that "not one of His bones shall be broken";* [37]and the Hebrew Scriptures also say, "They will look upon Him whom they pierced."*

[38]After all this, Joseph of Arimathea, a disciple who kept his faith a secret for fear of the Jewish officials, made a request to Pilate for the body of Jesus. Pilate granted his request, and Joseph retrieved the body. [39]Nicodemus, who first came to Jesus under the cloak of darkness, brought over 100 pounds of myrrh and ointments for His burial. [40]Together, they took Jesus' body and wrapped Him in linens soaked in essential oils and spices, according to Jewish burial customs.

[41]Near the place He was crucified, there was a garden with a newly prepared tomb. [42]Because it was the day of preparation, they arranged to lay Jesus in this tomb so they could rest on the Sabbath.

V

As the lifeless body of Jesus is laid into the virgin tomb, those who witnessed the spectacle retreat into the city that has claimed the lives of so many prophets. All are crushed that their teacher and friend has died such a horrible

---

* 19:24 Psalm 22:18 * 19:36 Exodus 12:46; Numbers 9:12; Psalm 34:20 * 19:37 Zechariah 12:10

death. Their hopes are dashed against the rocks of Golgotha. In the first hours of grief, Jesus' followers huddle together in secret in the city, hoping to avoid arrests and executions. They mourn. They grieve. They remember. Three days later, some venture outside the city and return to the place where He was buried. Miraculously, the stone has been rolled back, and the rock-hewn tomb is empty. Has someone taken His body? Are His enemies laying a trap for His followers? Or perhaps—could it be—that the last days have arrived?

20 Before the sun had risen on Sunday morning, Mary Magdalene made a trip to the tomb where His body was laid to rest. In the darkness, she discovered the covering had been rolled away. ²She darted out of the garden to find Simon Peter and the dearly loved disciple to deliver this startling news.

Mary Magdalene: They have taken the body of our Lord, and we cannot find Him!

³Together, they all departed for the tomb to see for themselves. ⁴They began to run, and Peter could not keep up. The beloved disciple arrived first ⁵but did not go in. There was no corpse in the tomb, only the linens and cloths He was wrapped in. ⁶When Simon Peter finally arrived, he went into the tomb and observed the same: ⁷the cloth that covered His face appeared to have been folded carefully and placed, not with the linen cloths, but to the side. ⁸After Peter pointed this out, the other disciple (who had arrived long before Peter) also entered the tomb; and based on what he saw, faith began to well up inside him! ⁹Before this moment, none of them understood the Scriptures and why He must be raised from the dead. ¹⁰Then they all went to their homes.
¹¹Mary, however, stood outside the tomb sobbing, crying, and kneeling at its entrance. ¹²As she cried, two heavenly messengers appeared before her sitting where Jesus' head and feet had been laid.

Heavenly Messengers: ¹³Dear woman, why are you weeping?

Mary Magdalene: They have taken away my Lord, and I cannot find Him.

¹⁴After uttering these words, she turned around to see Jesus standing before her, but she did not recognize Him.

Jesus: ¹⁵Dear woman, why are you sobbing? Who is it you are looking for?

She still had no idea who it was before her. Thinking He was the gardener, she muttered:

Mary Magdalene: Sir, if you are the one who carried Him away, then tell me where He is and I will retrieve Him.

Jesus: ¹⁶Mary!

Mary Magdalene (*turning to Jesus and speaking in Hebrew*): Rabboni, my Teacher!

Jesus: ¹⁷Mary, you cannot hold Me. I must rise above this world to be with My Father, who is also your Father; My God, who is also your God. Go tell this to all My brothers.

¹⁸Mary Magdalene obeyed and went directly to His disciples.

The hope of resurrection has often been a topic on the lips of Jesus. Now it is taking shape. Confusion gives way to conviction as Jesus appears alive over the next few Sundays. One by one He convinces His followers that God has raised Him from the dead.

Mary Magdalene (*announcing to the disciples*): I have seen the Lord, and this is what He said to me . . .

¹⁹On that same evening (Resurrection Sunday), the followers gathered together behind locked doors in fear that some of the Jewish leaders in Jerusalem were still searching for them. Out of nowhere, Jesus appeared in the center of the room.

Jesus: May each one of you be at peace.

²⁰As He was speaking, He revealed the wounds in His hands and side. The disciples

began to celebrate as it sank in that they were really seeing the Lord.

Jesus: [21]I give you the gift of peace. In the same way the Father sent Me, I am now sending you.

[22]Now He drew close enough to each of them that *they could feel His breath.* He breathed on them:

Jesus: Welcome the Holy Spirit of the living God. [23]You now have the mantle of God's forgiveness. As you go, you are able to share the life-giving power to forgive sins, or to withhold forgiveness.

[24]All of the eleven were present with the exception of Thomas. [25]He heard the accounts of each brother's interaction with the Lord.

The Other Disciples: We have seen the Lord!

Thomas: Until I see His hands, feel the wounds of the nails, and put my hand to His side, I won't believe what you are saying.

[26]Eight days later, they gathered again behind locked doors; and Jesus reappeared. This time Thomas was with them.

Jesus: May each one of you be at peace.

[27]He drew close to Thomas.

Jesus: Reach out and touch Me. See the punctures in My hands; reach out your hand, and put it to My side; leave behind your faithlessness, and believe.

Thomas (*filled with emotion*): [28]You are the one True God and Lord of my life.

Jesus: [29]Thomas, you have faith because you have seen Me. Blessed are all those who never see Me and yet they still believe.

[30]Jesus performed many other wondrous signs that are not written in this book. [31]These accounts are recorded so that you, too, might believe that Jesus is the Anointed, *the Liberating King,* the Son of God, because believing grants you the life He came to share.

21 There was one other time when Jesus appeared to the disciples—this time by the Sea of Tiberias. This is how it happened: [2]Simon Peter, Thomas (the Twin), Nathanael (the Galilean from Cana), the sons of Zebedee, and two other disciples were together.

Simon Peter (*to disciples*): [3]I am going fishing.

Disciples: Then we will come with you.

After Jesus' death, the disciples don't know what to do with themselves, other than return to their old livelihood of fishing. This band of fishermen is lost and lonely, but just when they think things can't be stranger, Jesus shows up. He tells them to fish on the other side of the boat. They do, and they are suddenly overwhelmed with fish. The nets are bulging.

What He shows here is that not only will their old ways of living leave His followers as empty as the nets, but their old habits will not work either. He has impacted their lives in a way that changed them forever. They can't go back. And He knows they don't know how to go forward.

They went out in the boat and caught nothing through the night. [4]As day was breaking, Jesus was standing on the beach; but they did not know it was Jesus.

Jesus: [5]My sons, you haven't caught any fish, have you?

Disciples: No.

Jesus: [6]Throw your net on the starboard side of the boat, and your net will find the fish.

They did what He said, and suddenly they could not lift their net because of the massive weight of the fish that filled it. [7]The disciple loved by Jesus turned to Peter and said:

Beloved Disciple: It is the Lord.

Immediately, when Simon Peter heard these words, he threw on his shirt (which he would take off while he was working) and dove into the sea. [8]The rest of the disciples followed him, bringing in the boat and dragging in their net full of fish. They were close to the shore, fishing only about 100 yards out. [9]When they arrived on shore, they saw a charcoal fire laid with fish on the grill. *He had* bread too.

Jesus *(to disciples)*: [10]Bring some of the fish you just caught.

[11]Simon Peter went back to the boat to unload the fish from the net. He pulled 153 large fish from the net. Despite the number of the fish, the net held without a tear.

Jesus: [12]Come, and join Me for breakfast.

V

Jesus reveals to His disciples a world where God is intimately involved, the main actor in the drama of history. These fish, all 153, are a sign from God representing the community of men and women transformed by faith. Some of them sit down and don't say a word as they ponder all of this. Others busy themselves in work. Each in his own way thinks, wonders, and prays.

That's how John always begins and ends his stories of Jesus: reminding believers to become the sons of God. The resurrection of Jesus shows the world He is the resurrection and the life. That isn't life after death; it is the reality that through Jesus believers can have abundant life, a full and meaningful life, here and now through faith.

Not one of the disciples dared to ask, "Who are You?" They knew it was the Lord. [13]Jesus took the bread and gave it to each of them, and then He did the same with the fish. [14]This was the third time the disciples had seen Jesus since His death and resurrection. [15]They finished eating breakfast.

Jesus: Simon, son of John, do you love Me more than these other things?

Simon Peter: Yes, Lord. You know that I love You.

Jesus: Take care of My lambs.

[16]Jesus asked him a second time . . .

Jesus: Simon, son of John, do you love Me?

Simon Peter: Yes, Lord. You must surely know that I love You.

Jesus: Shepherd My sheep.
[17](for the third time) Simon, son of John, do you love Me?

Peter was hurt because He asked him the same question a third time, "Do you love Me?"

Simon Peter: Lord, You know everything! You know that I love You.

Jesus: Look after My sheep. [18]I tell you the truth: when you were younger, you would pick up and go wherever you pleased; but when you grow old, someone else will help you and take you places you do not want to go.

V

Ever since the night Judas betrayed Jesus and Peter denied knowing Christ three times, Peter has felt small. He has felt he betrayed Jesus too. Matching the three denials, Jesus has Peter reaffirm his love for Him three times. At the same time, Jesus reaffirms Peter's call to ministry each time by challenging him to serve as a leader. The conversation on the beach that day affects him profoundly. From then on, Simon Peter is one of the most humble followers of Jesus, but he is also one of the great leaders of the early church, as Acts explains.

The disciples all learn a lesson that day. No matter what someone may have done, the Master wants the miracle of forgiveness to restore that person to be whom He made and called him or her to be.

[19]Jesus said all this as an indicator of the nature of Peter's death, which would glorify God. After this conversation, Jesus said,

Jesus: Follow Me!

[20]Peter turned around to see the disciple loved by Jesus following the two of them, the same disciple who leaned back on Jesus' side during their supper and asked, "Lord, who is going to betray You?"

Peter: [21]Lord, and what will happen to this man?

Jesus: [22]If I choose for him to remain till I return, what difference will this make to you? You follow Me!

[23]It is from this exchange with Jesus that some thought this disciple would not die. But Jesus never said that. He said, "If I choose for him to remain till I return, what difference will this make to you?" [24]That very same disciple is the one offering this truthful account written just for you. [25]There are so many other things that Jesus said and did; and if these accounts were also written down, the books could not be contained in the entire cosmos.

V

John has reached the end of his story. Future believers will go on without him, but not without his words. John's voice is added to the voices of the prophets and the witnesses declaring God has become flesh as Jesus, who manifested true life in the midst of humanity. Now that's a pretty big idea for a fisherman, but John goes to his grave bearing witness that it is true.

This account, in particular, shows how to enter into God's kingdom through faith in Jesus so they can experience eternal life. This is his invitation to join him in this marvelous journey.
